LET LOVE IN 101

A Practical Guide to Love & Happiness

By Jody Agard

Copyright

LET LOVE IN 101; A Practical Guide to Love and Happiness.

Copyright© 2015 by Jody Agard.

Author photograph by Steph Jones Photography StephJonesPhotography.com
Editing by Phillip Mygatt
Book Cover Design by Monique Nelson

Dedication

In loving memory of my dad, Donald Agard.

Contents

Acknowledgments

I dedicate this book to you, mom. I would not be who I am today without your unconditional love, wisdom and encouragement. You've been the angel in my life. In my darkest hours, you have been my light. Thank you for always being there and helping me to pick up the pieces of my life every step of the way. Thank you for being both a mother and a father to Jeff and I for all these years. Words cannot express my love, respect and adoration I have for you. I love you.

To my loving fiancé, thank you for your everlasting love. Thank you for believing in me and cheering me on. Thank you for your ongoing support, encouragement and patience. Thank you for pushing me to share my writings with the world. You continue to bring out the best in me; I love you to the moon and back.

To my handsome boys, thank you for understanding and giving me the space to write this book. I love you both so much.

To my friend and editor, Phil….thank you for all you have done to make this book possible. I appreciate your expertise, your friendship and your belief in me.

To my beautiful soul sisters; Jen, Kristin, and Amy…thank you for the laughs, the tears, the support and of course, your {sisterhood} friendship.

Lastly, thank you dad for the love, the laughs, and the wisdom you gave me in the fifteen years I was blessed to have you in my life and for the divine guidance you continue to give me. Thank you for being the "The wind beneath my wings".

The Back Story

The first man I ever fell in love with was my dad, as most daughters do. I adored my dad. He was all the things a daughter yearned for in a father; loving, kind, gentle, giving, attentive and fun. I'd say I had a very "normal" childhood. I was tucked in at night, we ate dinner together, took family vacations together, went to church…the whole nine yards. When I was thirteen years old, after eighteen years of marriage, my parents separated for reasons I was unsure of at the time.

At first, I was sad when my dad sat me down to explain they were separating but I also knew this wouldn't change my relationship with my dad.

In fact, we became closer.

During their two-year separation I spent a lot of time with my dad. We talked on the phone nearly every day, he'd pick me up from school and I looked forward to going to his house, especially on the weekends. As most teenagers did, I also loved hanging with my friends, so I'd often just bring my girlfriends along with me. They adored my dad.

We'd go to the movies together, we'd take road trips to Connecticut to spend time with his family, we'd go hiking through the woods, we'd go to the mall and then there were those nights my dad and I were happy to just snuggle on the couch and watch movies together.

On May 22 1992 and one week before my parent's divorce was going to be final, my life was turned upside down.

I was 15 years old and as I sat in front of the long mirror that hung behind my closet door, I attempted to put my hair up in a bun for my gymnastics class.

I was in a hurry and knew my friends parents would arrive soon.

Unexpectedly, I heard my mom's voice shout from the bottom of the stairwell "Kids, I need you to come downstairs please."

I was confused why she was home from work so early, but I didn't think too much of it. I was mostly annoyed that she was interrupting me.

"Hang on a minute" my brother and I both shouted back.

After her third request, we finally obliged and made our way down the stairs both anxious to get on with it.

We turned the corner into the dining room.

I took one glance at my mother's face standing by the breakfast nook in the kitchen and I *knew* something had gone terribly wrong.

We approached her *"Its your father."*

Without even knowing what I was saying at the time, the words *"He committed suicide didn't he?"* came flying out of my mouth.

{Still to this day, I have no idea where those words came from.}

She pulled me close to her "I'm so sorry honey."

Although I may have said the words, I was utterly *unprepared* for her confirmation that my dad did in fact take his own life.

The pain I felt in my heart was indescribable.

My whole world came crashing down before me.

Everything I had known, loved, and trusted was shattered into a zillion little pieces and there wasn't a thing I could do about it.

He didn't leave a suicide note, leaving many unanswered questions.

To say I felt a void in my heart was an *understatement*.

To put simply, I was lost and heartbroken.

I wanted nothing more than for the pain to just "go away".

The days and nights ahead were long and painful.

I spent the first five years crying myself to sleep as I clutched his sweatshirt each night, desperately praying for my pain to end. I had no idea how I would live without my dad.

Eventually, the tears did finally come to an end.

As I lay in bed one evening, I realized I had gone an entire day without shedding a tear. (This was no easy feat considering at least once a day I would burst into tears and cry uncontrollably.) In that very moment, I felt like I got my life back. I vividly remember saying to myself

"Thank God! I made it! If I can get through that, I can get through *anything* in life!"

Although I felt I had reached a point where I was finally starting to accept life without Dad, I also began to shut down emotionally. Looking back, I can clearly see the walls I began building around my heart. I became "strong". I was told I had "thick skin" and I was "tough".

I had officially entered "survival mode" (a protective mechanism, comparable to the fight or flight response, only on a deep emotional level). It was in this mode that I could no longer cry. It didn't matter how sad a movie was, it didn't matter what words were said or not said to me. It didn't matter who died. No matter how hard I tried (and I *tried*), I could not bring myself to cry.

There were many times over the years I *wanted* and *needed* to cry, but I just couldn't.

My ex-husband used to tell me my tear ducts were broken. I didn't want to believe it back then though.

I had a friend once tell me *"I wish I was strong like you, I hate being so emotional."* I remember saying, *"I wish I could feel and be more sensitive like you."*

I didn't want to have thick skin. I wanted to cry, I wanted to feel again. I wanted to believe in love and in the "happily ever after" again. I wanted to be vulnerable and put down my walls for that special someone. I wanted to fall in love with the *nice guy*. But, I just couldn't seem to bring myself to soften the way I needed to soften to be able to acquire these things.

For a long time, I felt as though more than just my tear ducts were broken.

I felt my whole being was damaged.

I felt fragmented because I couldn't cry or bring myself to truly open my heart.

I thought something was wrong with me.

In my eyes, I was "broken".

Only now do I realize I wasn't "broken", I just needed to love myself and allow love to come into my life.

Yep. I'm talking about that little thing called "self-love".

Growing up, I attended Catholic school.

Looking back, that was the reoccurring theme I remember hearing from the nuns, teachers, and my parents.

"Love yourself."

The problem (as I saw it) was, we were never taught what "loving yourself" looked like.

This left me wondering what the true meaning of self-love was. How does that translate in the "real world", how is "loving yourself" applied into everyday life? What does it look like in practical terms? When I'd ask these questions, I always seemed to get the old standby answers... "Respect yourself. Respect your body. Stand up for what you believe"...blah blah blah!

Over the course of my life, I knew there was more to the generic answers my friends and family gave me. At least I *hoped* that would be the case anyway.

For nineteen years after my dad's suicide, I felt like I was asleep in so many ways. Without even realizing it, I was so oblivious and disconnected from who I really was. I've been told that was "normal" after experiencing a traumatic event such as suicide. Although unaware, I was in survival mode.

Eyes Wide Open

When I finally began to "wake-up" to life as I call it, I was feeling unfulfilled in my career, my relationship was falling apart, and I was feeling overwhelmed raising two boys as a single mom.

I was financially unstable, and working well over 40 hours/week & busting my ass just trying to keep my head above water.

I was hardly "living" at all and I so desperately wanted more out of life.

I realized I was walking in the same footsteps as my dad. The only difference was while I chose to live, I wasn't truly "living".

I wanted to feel fulfilled and my life to have more meaning.

I was utterly exhausted and becoming less-and-less tolerant. I became more-and-more annoyed with everybody around me.

The littlest things would annoy me, which wasn't really like me. Even after my dad's suicide, I was generally a positive, fun, outgoing, and loving person.

I started to notice my behavior and began saying to myself "this isn't like me".

I knew my circumstances weren't going to change overnight. I also knew I had to be the one to make changes, which ultimately *forced* me to really look at my life.

When I peeked inside at all the parts of me that I tried so hard to push down, I realized I had to make some serious changes and work from the inside out.

This was when my real soul searching began.

I was led me back to the same question I had been asking myself years before. *"How do I love myself?"* I began asking myself this question over-and-over again. Only this time, I was determined to find the answers.

Today, twenty-two years after my dad's suicide, I'm happy to report that I have found those answers and what self-love really means.

(At least to me anyway.)

My walls have come crashing down which has caused me to become softer on the inside as well as on the outside. I stop to smell the roses more, I appreciate my kids more, I'm more accepting of myself and others, and I'm more apt to be vulnerable and express myself authentically.

More than anything else though, I'm more patient and understanding of myself and others.

In all honestly, I've become quite the mush-ball, especially when it comes to love. I'm engaged to one of the most gentle, loving, caring men I know, Josh. He continues to bring out the best in me.

Now please, don't get me wrong, I'm not saying our relationship has been all lollipops, unicorns, and butterflies; we have had our ups and downs for sure. But, I'm realizing more-and-more that in fact the beauty of all relationships is that they have the opportunity to push us into becoming who we truly are (or who we are not).

My life has been transformed because of one thing and one thing only…

That one thing

I began loving myself.

That's it.

When I started doing more of *that*, my entire life improved!

I've learned through experience that self-love is the prerequisite to all healthy relationships too.

This is what this book is all about, the process and journey I went through to become more loving; to myself and others.

It's my hope through my story and tried-and-true techniques that you too can find that love in your heart that once existed so freely. Whether you are single, married or newly dating, these principles can be applied to you and to all areas of your life; relationships, career, health & even finances.

As I made my journey through my own personal heartbreak, pain, and misery, I discovered there wasn't one "magic button", one particular thing that helped me turn my life around and find true happiness; instead, there were many principles (revelations, in fact) that I came to call tools in my "toolbox" and I want to share those tools with you.

They are:

    1. Learning self-love and how that will lead you to happiness.
    2. Learning how to become self-aware.

3. Learning how to take charge of your own well-being.

4. Learning how to let go of your guilt.

5. Learning from others.

6. Learning how to be in the moment.

7. Learning how to see yourself through the eyes of others.

8. Learning how to forgive.

9. Learning how to overcome your fears.

If you apply these tools to your everyday life, I can guarantee that your life WILL become more joyous, meaningful and fulfilling, just like mine is today.

CHAPTER 1
Self-Love 101

We all experience unhappiness from time-to-time and all for varying reasons; some big and some small. In those underlying moments of unhappiness, I find it most interesting that half the time we don't even know *why* we're feeling unfulfilled and unhappy. Then, there are other times; we know exactly who or what is causing our unhappiness. Maybe it's the kids, our marriage, the finances, the lack of emotional support, or the endless hours we spend at work.

Let's talk about that underlying feeling of unhappiness for a moment.

Besides the normal ups-and-downs of life, maybe your life is going great. Maybe you're married to a person you love, the kids are doing great in school, you're surrounded by friends and family who love and support you, you have a stable career, your finances are in order and your health is intact.

Maybe overall, you feel blessed and know you have a lot to be grateful for.

Deep down though, there might be this uneasy feeling that *something* is missing. Maybe you're just not quite sure what it is. You may even find yourself thinking, "Knock it off, you have nothing to be unhappy about, stop being ungrateful…", so you blow it off and continue on the trek you were on…

Below, there may be a storm brewing.

Who are you?

I've played many roles in my life and I've had numerous professional titles over the course of my career. Currently, the professional titles I hold are; best-selling author, relationship coach, inspirational speaker, freelance writer, certified life coach, blogger, CEO, and everything else that comes with being an entrepreneur.

Some of the personal roles I currently play in my life are; mom, fiancé, daughter, sister, friend and aunt.

While these things make up who I'm perceived to be externally, there is much more to be told about who I am as a whole – a story that continues to evolve over time.

When we're introduced to a new person, the first thing our society has grown accustom to asking is "What do you do for a living?" As if what we do for work tells the story of who we are. I find it to be such an impersonal question and way too "surfacy".

Imagine if we learned to ask a question that would offer more depth; such as "How did you get to where you are today?" Now that would be revealing.

While mom, wife, husband, professional, friend, business owner…are essentially a *part* of who you are, that's not ALL of who you are. In fact, those definitions are simply a part of your personality. So, it's as if you're only telling *half* a story.

Two Sides of the Same Coin:

Dr. Wayne Dyer explains this concept beautifully in his book Wishes Fulfilled…

"Your higher self exists beyond that lower, false self. So begin to know yourself as something far greater than ever-changing, ever-dying aspects that have dominated your picture of who you are. Who am I? is then answered with, I am an infinite being who originated not from my parents, but from a Source that is itself birthless, deathless and changeless."

What if I told you there were two sides to you; your personality-self (ego or false-self) and your higher-self?

The one you're probably most familiar with is the personality side of you. This side contains your likes, dislikes and all your personality traits and characteristics. I.e. optimistic, outgoing, funny and shy, etc.

"When you were a kid, you dreamed big dreams and wanted great things for yourself."

The other part of you, your *higher-self*, contains all that the personality side wants to become. This "other side" of you is essentially a much BIGGER version of yourself.

For me, it's that part of me that *knows* (without a doubt) I can have, do and be anything I want to be. I was born with this knowledge.

When I was a kid, I dreamed big dreams and wanted great things for myself.

I was fearless and loved challenges. I was confident. I trusted. I didn't care how I looked. I was happy. I didn't care what people thought about me. If I felt like dancing, I danced. If I felt like crying, I cried. If I was tired, I slept. If I saw something funny, I laughed. I knew how to have fun. I lived in the present moment and not in the past or the future. I had no idea "failures" even existed and I most certainly didn't beat myself up when things didn't turn out right. I was persistent and resilient. I spoke my mind and shared my feelings. I loved freely. I smiled often.

I was just <u>me</u>.

You are no different.

The child in you didn't know how to be anything other than yourself. You were as authentic as they came and proud of who you were.

You too were 100% yourself when you were just a small child. You were happy being you because it felt natural.

This was your "authentic-self".

But then....life happened. As you got older and began to experience life's struggles, your personality-self (smaller version) started to dominant your "authentic" self. This is when you began comparing yourself to others, when you didn't measure up to "everybody else", you felt inferior. Although unaware, you began internally beating yourself up, telling self-limiting stories over-and-over in your head. You began to feel more-and-more insecure and embarrassed as time went on. The opinions of others began to really matter to you. You knew if you acted one way, "X" would happen. If you acted another way, "Y" would happen. You began to conform to the needs of the people around you. You began doing things to make everyone else happy, until eventually you lost sight of who you were. Slowly, you learned to turn your back on that larger part of you, (your higher-self) for the sake of others.

This was all done without you even being conscious of it.

It just kinda happened.

The good though is that your higher-self, meaning that bigger version of yourself never turns its back on you; it still exists within you today. In fact, it is seeking to come out and play!

Any unhappiness that you're feeling can actually be a really good thing.

Why?

Well, because when you know what you *don't* want, you become much clearer on all the things you <u>do</u> want.

Essentially, the missing things in your life are forcing you to look at the parts of yourself that have been pushed down and ignored for way too long.

Let's rewind and go back to my original question though "Who are you?"

Ok I'll be honest with you; this is kind of a trick question.

The answer actually lies in your ability to let go of who you are *not*?

You do that by stepping into who you are and reconnecting with the larger part of yourself.

Your "real" self.

That lack of fulfillment, disconnection and underlying unhappiness you may be feeling is a result of you becoming disconnected with who you *truly* are.

In my coaching practice, my writing, and public speaking, my main objective is to reconnect you to you by helping you let go of all the things you are not.

Life is a constant growth process. You are always evolving and changing.

What you may have wanted three years ago may not be what you want today though.

Maybe it's a job, a career, eating habits, or a relationship.

The disconnection occurs when we stay where we are because we're re afraid to grow with ourselves.

We claim we're "stuck".

Often though, we're not stuck. We know exactly what we need to do in order to get to where we want to go but we refuse to make the necessary changes.

Your happiness depends on your willingness to keep up....not with anybody else but yourself.

Be Selfish. Put Yourself First

"When our tanks are full and we feel balanced, we have the energy and patience to give love to the world around us and the people in it."

Like a car, in order for us to function properly and to feel centered, loving, and grounded, we need to be sure our inner tank is filled. Not with gas, but with <u>love</u>.

Self-love.

When our tanks are full and we feel balanced, we have the energy and patience to give love to the world around us and the people in it. When we are running on empty or even on low fumes, we feel overwhelmed, angry and bitter and this is how we end up treating those around us.

When we're unhappy, it becomes a knee-jerk reaction to immediately point fingers and blame our partners, friends, or even parents for our problems.

All our lives, we've heard the phrases "You make me so angry". Or, "He makes me so angry". "She pisses me off!" Until finally, we start believing that *other people* are responsible for our happiness and <u>they</u> have the *power* to determine how *we* feel.

We are mistaken when we blame our partners and those around us for our negative feelings; it's just the excuse we use because we feel bad about *ourselves*. Why do we do this? Because it's much easier to place blame on someone other than ourselves than it is to take responsibility, step out of our comfort zones, and take action to make the necessary changes.

But, until we recognize this as a *pattern* and understand that our unhappiness is a lack of **self-love**, our outside circumstances will never change and our relationships will never improve. If you've been pointing fingers at your partner or spouse for *your* unhappiness, understand the void you've been feeling was more than likely missing <u>long before</u> you even met your partner.

Self-love is vital for all loving, lasting, and healthy relationships.

When I began doing more of truly loving myself, my life drastically changed for the better.

Learning to Open Our Hearts

The summers in Florida are miserable. They're hot, humid, wet, and sticky. Usually by the end of August, you'll hear the Floridians begin to talk about how many days are left until the cooler weather arrives.

It was nearing the end of September and my son and I were taking the dogs out for a walk. Immediately, we noticed the first *tinge* of coolness in the morning air.

It felt so refreshing. We both agreed we were really looking forward to the fall and winter weather.

"How much longer until it gets cooler, Mom?"

"I don't know, hopefully in just a few more weeks."

"I can't wait until we can open up all the windows!"

I agreed.

Even though the humidity was back in full swing by 9am that morning, the brief crisp air was just what we needed. It gave us hope and reassurance that it was just around the corner. It was our light at the end of the tunnel.

The humidity is just something the residents of Florida learn to deal with. Errrrr, learn to avoid rather. We "deal" with the humidity the same way the northeasterner's "deal" with the cold and harsh winters. We hibernate. We lock ourselves inside our homes (or submerse ourselves in some type of body of water) until we can enjoy the weather outside.

A few weeks after our walk the weather forecasters were predicting our first snap of cool, mild weather for the upcoming weekend.

We were thrilled!

I jumped out of bed early Saturday morning as if it were Christmas morning. I ran to my bedroom window, put my hand on the glass to measure the temperature and sure enough, my window was nice and cool.

I ran downstairs, opened the front door and breathed in the fresh, crisp fall air. It felt so good.

I ran back inside, shut the air conditioner off, and opened up all the windows.

Since this was the first day of beautiful fall weather, Josh and I decided to take the dogs for a long walk. As we walked, we noticed more-and-more neighbors were opening up their windows as we made our way through the neighborhood.

We'd hear the clicks of the window locks being undone and the swooshing sound of the windows going up. And then, at last, we'd see our neighbors' smiling faces as they looked out their windows.

If only we could open our hearts as easily as we opened our windows, I thought to myself.

Imagine, not even thinking twice about unlocking our hearts and flinging them open despite our fears or hurts of the past. Imagine the happiness that would surround us. Imagine the love it would bring.

When I learned to open my heart as easily as I opened my windows, my relationships improved, I discovered my life purpose and my life finally began to fall into place.

I gained clarity, I started my own coaching practice, I began communicating more effectively (and lovingly), I began appreciating my family more and I began to forgive the people of my past. I even did something I never said I would do again....I got engaged.

{I also learned to never say never.}

I've come to realize we simply can't give what we don't have inside; if we don't have self-love and take care of ourselves, how can we possibly expect to be able to give love to others.

29

If we don't forgive ourselves, how can we ever expect to forgive others?

If we first and foremost, fill our own tank with unconditional love, compassion and understanding, *then* we can give those things to others.

I used to think the happiest people in the world were those who had everything; the money, the relationships, the time, the success, and the dream job. But, I know now that's a false sense of happiness and a common misbelief.

The happiest people in the world are actually those who are happy *regardless* of their circumstances; even the most challenging ones. This is why I developed my very own personal life motto:

"Life isn't about having a perfect life; it's about having the perfect tools for our imperfect lives."

Even though at times we can't control our outer circumstances, we <u>can</u> control our inner world and the way we think about things.

We can choose to look at the challenges in front of us as some sort of punishment <u>or</u> we can choose to believe in the possibility that we're being guided to something even *better*.

Some people think that because I'm a relationship coach and life coach, I'm always frolicking in the fields, doing cartwheels, and singing a little tune! (HAHA!) I can't help but laugh at the hideousness (and ignorance) of such assumptions.

Life happens. I'm human just like you.

Not only are humans imperfect, but we shouldn't expect our lives *not* to have challenges.

That's the beauty of life; we will *always* have challenges.

There will be ups and there will be downs.

I'm faced with challenges, I juggle, I'm pulled in ninety different directions, my kids challenge me, I have personal goals and deadlines to meet, I have my "off" days and I get cranky sometimes.

I also have tools and I use them daily as needed because my *happiness* depends on them.

So nowadays, those off days are often few and far between.

I know if I don't pay close attention to the way I feel though — to my energy levels, my moods and my thoughts — it would be easy for me to fall off the wagon.

I also have a daily practice of taking preventative measures rather than simply putting out fires as they come. That's the key; preventative measures

So, without further ado, here are a few tools for *your* toolbox. These tools are proven to work. They have not only changed *my* life, but they have also changed each and every one of my clients' lives. *Disclaimer: In order for the tools to work, you must use them.* The handyman who refuses to pick up his hammer will always miss a day's work. It isn't the tool that does the work; it's the operator willing to pick it up. While some tools may seem simple and obvious, others may seem pointless. Use them anyway. Simplicity and practicality are <u>key</u>.

CHAPTER 2
Notice What You're Noticing

Whether I'm coaching a client one-on-one, doing a group coaching session, or speaking to college kids or corporate leaders....this is always where I start.

We can't change anything until we are first aware; simply notice what you're noticing.

We tend to go through our lives on auto-pilot. Half the time, we don't even notice where our attention is. Our mind is just spinning, ranting about this and raving about that. We have this voice inside our heads that chatters and carries on-and-on about all the many fears, worries, and stresses we have. You know the voice I'm talking about. It's that inner voice that always has something to say like the teenager who "doesn't know when to shut up". Sometimes the voice has nice things to say and other times it only notices all the things that are going wrong in our lives. It's always there, always saying something though. That voice especially likes to talk while we're doing mindless tasks such as driving, brushing our teeth, taking a shower, making dinner, walking through a parking lot, or sitting in the waiting room of a doctor's office.

Just take notice the next time you're doing any of these things.

Inner peace starts with controlling that voice and no longer allowing it to control you and the way you live or love.

Here are some examples of what your inner voice might say to you:

- {As you get out of the shower you notice your naked body}…*Ewe I'm so fat, I'll always be fat. Diets never work. I must get it from Mom.*
- *I'll never get that promotion, I should just stay where I am; it's comfortable here. I'm not good at interviews anyway.*
- *Ugh, I never have any time to myself.*
- *I'm never going to have time to finish all my work.*
- *My husband is such a jerk. He never helps me.*
- *I wish I'd get more help around here! I'm always doing everything for everybody else!*

Those are just a few. I could go on-and-on. It may even be happening right now as you are reading this book… *"What am I doing? I shouldn't be reading right now. I don't have time for this. I need to be doing the dishes…"* (Ignore it and just keep reading)

So notice what you're noticing. Are you only noticing the negative things in your life or are you noticing the positive things and feeling grateful for them too? Where are you putting your attention? If you're mainly focusing on all the negative things, your mood and emotions will reflect just that. The good news is if you're mostly focusing on the good you have in your life, your mood and emotions will reflect that instead.

When my inner tank is running low, I can get really bitchy, irritable, and grumpy. That's when a red flag goes up, an indicator that it's time to check in with myself to see when was the last time I did something for myself and took a much needed break. If I can't remember the last time, then that's my answer. So now, thanks to my mood...I'm *aware*. But, simply being aware won't change anything. The next step for me is to actually do something about it and use one of my trusted tools to pull myself out of it.

Action Step: Literally listen to yourself as you go about your day. Pay attention to your inner chatter today.

CHAPTER 3
Your Happiness Is Up To You

Be in charge of your own well-being! Don't ever expect anyone other than yourself to stand up for *your* well-being. That is an unrealistic expectation.

If you're waiting for your partner or kids to say "Hey, why don't you take the night off, I'll take care of things tonight?" don't hold your breath. Not only will you possibly be waiting for a very long time, you may be becoming uber-resentful in the meantime. Resentment isn't good. It weighs us down and depletes our moods and energy levels.

It's unfair to put those kinds of expectations on other people too. The only person who knows it's time for a break is *you,* and you have to be willing to first admit it to yourself and later communicate your needs to those around you.

> *"Self-love is about knowing and honoring your needs, wants, and wishes."*

It's about understanding your own inner world, including your thoughts and feelings. It's about being kind and compassionate with yourself.

To create long-lasting success in any area of your life, whether it is in your relationships, health, career or finances…you <u>must</u> have balance in your life. While having "perfect" balance is a myth, you can strive to improve the balance of your well-being. If you're working 80+ hours a week skipping lunches and rarely able to see your family, and then ask yourself… *Am I really <u>living</u> a quality life or am I simply blasting through life?*

You must do whatever it takes to do things that will fill your inner tank. Make it a priority and stop waiting for other people to give you permission to take a break. (If you need someone to give you permission, consider this book your permission.)

Something else you can do for yourself is to stop trying to be some sort of super-hero. You're not. You are human. You need breaks.

It's time to start dabbling in the activities you once loved to do for yourself, but have put on the back-burner.

What are they?

Painting? Scrapbooking? Writing? Skiing? Snowboarding? Photography? Yoga? Hiking? Running? Baking? Cooking? Kick Boxing?

What types of things do you or did you once enjoy?

(The harder it is for you to recall your favorite pastimes, the more disconnected you may have become from your inner-self.)

If you keep digging, the answers will come.

I can hear you saying *"Even if I can recall them, I've got kids and a family now. It's not like I can just get up and go explore old and new hobbies whenever I want."*

Really?

Who says?

Sure, it might take some planning. But it certainly can be done.

Start small. Commit to just once a month at first. Put it on the calendar. Do something for yourself that you truly enjoy, an activity that "fills your cup".

Gradually, you can increase to twice a month or even weekly. Line up those babysitters if you have to.

Do whatever it takes to take care of yourself and encourage your partner to do the same.

You will find the more you take care of yourself, the better you'll take care of those around you.

I found that the more I did things for myself, even if it was just take a quiet bath, the things that once pushed my buttons, no longer got to me.

You too will find you're more patient, tolerant, and understanding of those around you.

Be willing to say *"Hey. I need a break. Do you think you could handle the kids for me tonight (or tomorrow) while I have some alone time?"* Don't expect anyone to read your mind, especially your partner and most certainly not your kids.

CHAPTER 4
Shedding the Guilt

Let go of the GUILT.

Now!

----That's an order.

When it comes to doing things for ourselves, we become our own worst enemy.

We place all these unrealistic expectations on ourselves and then we beat ourselves up for not being able to meet them. As much as we'd love to think otherwise, again, we are *not* super-hero action figures.

I find women operate on a great deal of guilt, especially moms. It's partly our own fault because we have this "it's easier to do it ourselves" mentality. Although we have good intentions, this is our way of trying to control everything around us. However, this mentality doesn't come without a price.

Doing something for ourselves can often translate into "I'm being a "bad" mom/wife" if I don't do this or that. We try to convince ourselves that we shouldn't want or need to take a breather, so we power through life. We have this preconceived notion that marriage and family equates to giving every ounce of our being to our children, partners, extended family, careers, and essentially sacrificing our own lives and well-being.

While this may have been the case in the 1950's, we're in the twenty-first century so get rid of that old way of living the same way you got rid of your old Blackberry. Allow your partners and children to get more involved in the daily duties.

I'm going to assume that you've probably been on an airplane at least once in your life...

If you have, then you should know the first thing the flight attendants tell us when they're going through their safety procedures...

*"In the event that the plane loses cabin pressure while at altitude, the oxygen masks will drop. Help children and others with their masks only **after** yours are secure."*

Imagine yourself on such a plane, traveling with your children or grandchildren, nieces or nephews. The hatches above the seat open and the masks fall. Your natural instinct would be to get the masks on your children and then help *yourself*. At first, doing anything but that would seem selfish, wouldn't it?

So why do the airlines advise us to do it this way? Is it because they don't care about children and elderly?

Quite the contrary actually; they know you simply **can't** help *anybody* if you're unconscious, or worse, dead. The airlines want to

41

ensure you can help as many people as you possibly can, which can only be done after helping yourself *first*.

Try applying this very same principle to your own life. Yes. I'm telling you to put yourself FIRST! Yes, I'm telling you to put yourself *before* your family, before your career, and before your community.

Here's why—

You might *think* you're being a good mom, dad, wife, husband, aunt, uncle, friend, or daughter by pushing through life and all the things that come with it, but you can't possibly be all those things if you're burnt out and stressed to the max. You just can't. It's unrealistic.

As a matter of fact, you may not believe me, but you'll be a *better* mom, dad, employee, wife, CEO, brother, uncle, sister, business owner, or friend by taking time out for *yourself*.

Logically, you may think spending more hours at the office and working through lunches will produce more work, but that's not always so. If you're tired and drained, the quality of your work will suffer and you'll actually be much less productive. On the flip side, if you take breaks and you allow yourself the time to rejuvenate, refresh, and restart your engines, not only will you get more done in *less* time, but the quality will subsequently improve.

It's a win-win.

I know; it seems counter-productive.

I thought so too, at first.

Like you, I pushed through life in hopes of getting more done. In all honesty, my default is *still* to push through life; go-go-go and do-do-do.

We don't ever truly shed the defaults of our personalities; we just learn to work with them.

That's why it's so important to simply become aware. In order to change anything in my life, I have to first catch myself doing it, and then change behaviors if it isn't serving me well.

My life changed immensely and continues to improve because I'm more aware of my thoughts. I realized that I needed to stop trying to control my outer circumstances and instead, direct my thoughts in a more positive manner.

Since I "woke up" from my deep sleep, many would say that I completely changed.

Really though, I'm still me, only now I'm just a bigger version of myself.

I'm still goofy (and sometimes ditzy) little old me. I'm just much more aware of who I'm *not*.

Ignoring my own needs because of guilt is the working of my personality. It's in my nature to blast through my day. I'm aware of this now more than ever.

With my awareness comes a choice for me to do something about it. (Or not.) It's my responsibility to begin living the way I would love to live, regardless of my circumstances.

I know if I want to stay balanced, I have to pay very close attention to my self-talk, my actions, and my feelings.

It takes work. I constantly battle that so-called, logical part of my brain that says things like *"A FIFTEEN MINUTE WALK IN THE MIDDLE OF THE DAY... ARE YOU NUTS? GET YOUR ASS BACK INSIDE AND GET BACK TO WORK! YOU ARE BEING ANYTHING BUT PRODUCTIVE RIGHT NOW! GET BACK TO WORK!"* It's the voice that tries to convince me that I'd be more productive sitting at the computer, pushing through my work, pushing through my exhaustion, and even pushing through my hunger.

CHAPTER 5
Balancing Your Day

I was in Corporate America for over twelve years, so I worked the typical 9am-5pm day.

Well, more like 7am-7pm working through lunch because I couldn't stand to leave things on my desk, meticulous, perfectionist, workaholic, type of hours actually.

For many of those years, I was a single mom. The boys went to their dad's every other weekend, so during the week it was all me. I was exceptionally blessed to have my mom to help me when I needed her to. Back then though, I thought I was super-woman! Often, I would wait until I was on the verge of a breakdown before asking her for any help.

In order to get my kids from daycare and afterschool on time, precision timing was a must. I had it down to a science.

This was my schedule (before I "woke-up" to life):

Time:	Duty:
5:00 AM	Hit the snooze at least 5 times
5:00 AM - 5:30	Drag my ass out of bed, jump in the shower half asleep
5:30-6:15 am	Shower, get ready and hope the kids don't hear me
6:15-7:00 am	Get the youngest up first, then the oldest. Various roles include; chef, referee, mediator, drill sergeant, mother and maid
7:00-7:15 am	Throw kids in car and race to the oldest's before - care program
7:15-7:35 am	Race to my youngest daycare – drop off
7:35-8:15 am	Cigarettes! 35 of them. Enjoy the silence, but hate the traffic and slow drivers (those that were doing the speed limit).
8:15-8:25 am	Arrive in the parking lot, take off my layered "smoking shirt" (So I don't smell like I just left a bar), body spray, gum, lip-gloss, smile, game face. Check! Say quick hello's, turn on

my computer, put lunch in fridge and sit at my desk.

8:25-2:30 pm	Work, work, work, work.
2:30-5:01 pm	Feeling nauseous and suddenly realize I forgot to eat lunch. Grab my lunch from fridge and nibble while I continue to work.
5:01 - 5:11 pm	Finish emails, shut everything down, pack up and dash out the door.
5:11 - 6:00 pm	Pick up kids at individual destinations. Throw kids back in the car and race home.
6:00 -8:00 pm	Various roles include: chef, referee, mediator, drill sergeant, mother and maid.
8:00 - 10 pm	Tuck kids into bed, skip over pages in books, and then clean up the tornado that just blew through the house.
10 - 11 pm	Wash makeup off (most of the time), brush teeth, attempt to watch tv, pass out.
Next Day:	REPEAT

I had moments where I truly enjoyed the boys, but most of the time I felt like a robotic drill sergeant rather than embracing each moment as a mother.

I did this day-in-and- day-out until one day I heard myself. It was one of those weird aha-moments. I mean, I **really** heard myself! I always had a positive outlook on life and more often than not, I remained positive about the cards I was dealt. But, when I took a step back in this particular moment, I suddenly realized I was snapping at the boys more, I was short-fused, I had less-and-less tolerance for even the normal horse play amongst the boys, and even the smallest things bothered me.

At that very moment, I decided I had enough. I realized I was burnt out. I knew something had to change. I knew the pace I was going wasn't good for me or my boys. I desperately wanted a smooth running household and a smooth running mindset. I knew I'd be insane if I continued the pace I was going, expecting a different outcome. That's hideous and insane!

New Beginnings:

At first, I began making small changes. I knew I had to be realistic and practical about my changes, otherwise I'd fall off the wagon.

Even though making changes at first felt selfish, I reminded myself that the boys would be appreciative of their new mommy who would emerge from feeling balanced and reset and that's exactly what happened.

Below is my revised schedule. You'll find no major changes; just some tweaks.

New Schedule - Day one -

Time: **Duty:**

5:00 AM   Rise and Shine! Stretch. Thank God I opened my eyes this morning.

5:00-6:00   Sit for 5-10 minutes to read a few pages of my book and drink my tea. Enjoy my shower while focusing on; what a productive day I was going to have. Pay attention to my internal talk. Enjoy the process of getting dressed, applying my make-up and going about my morning.

6:00-7:00   Get the youngest up first, then the oldest. Various roles include; chef, referee, mediator, mother and maid

7:00-7:15   Give the boys a 10 minute warning that the "bus" is leaving. Chat and enjoy my precious time while we drop the oldest off at his beforecare program.

7:15-7:35   Chat and enjoy my precious time while taking my youngest to daycare

7:35-8:15 am	Less cigarettes and more self-help cd's. Shifted my perspective about the traffic and looked at it as an opportunity to self-educate myself.
8:15-8:25 am	Arrive in the parking lot, take off my layered "smoking shirt" (So I don't smell like I just left a bar), body spray, gum, lip-gloss, smile, game face. Check! Say quick hello's, turn on my computer, put lunch in fridge and sit at my desk.
8:25-10:30 am	Work
10:30 - 10:45 am	Walked around the building, sometimes with a cigarette, sometimes not. (within 6 months I quit smoking--simply because...I just didn't want them anymore. They suddenly grossed me out.)
10:45-1:00 pm	Work, work. Deep breaths. Work. Deep breaths.
1:00-1:30 pm	Lunch, most times still ate at my desk.
1:30-3:45 pm	Work, work. Deep breaths. Work. Deep breaths.
3:45-4:00 pm	Getting antsy. Go into the bathroom to take my new "smoke-break" and do some yoga

stretches. Let co-workers assume I'm having stomach issues.

4:00 - 5:11 pm	Wrap things up, finish emails, shut everything down, pack up and head out the door (feeling way more productive somehow).
5:11 - 6:00 pm	Pick each child up at their destinations.
6:00- 6:15 pm	Tell the boys (ages 12 & 5) that they can unload their backpacks and then sit quietly on the couch and read while they wait for me to come out. Go into my bedroom, lock the door and do one of the following: A.) Sit quietly on my bed, taking a few deep breaths. B.) Sit in my closet, taking a few deep breaths. C.) Take a quick shower. D.) Read a few pages of a book, any book. E.) Skimmed through a few pages of my favorite magazine.
6:15- 8:00 pm	Same tasks, same roles, only with an improved temperament.
8:00 - 8:30 pm	Put kids to bed, read all the pages of books.
9:30 - 10:30 pm	Pick up the house, get ready for bed, read.

10:30- 10:45 pm   Just before passing out, I'd close my eyes and focus on two things: 1) On any good points of my day (even if it was just one small tiny thing) 2.) Set my intentions and focus on having

51

a great day tomorrow, picture my commute into work, my meetings, my entire day, going good.

Next Day: REPEAT

As you see, I didn't do anything drastic. The key is to not let it feel like an overwhelming commitment, but a great first step. I tend to put too many expectations on myself, so for once I decided to give myself a break and just do what was comfortable. I had to walk before I could run. I knew if I jumped right into attempting to meditate for an hour, I'd quit by the end of the week. I've always been the type to do things on my own terms. However, I don't believe that everyone fits into the same exact box.

So what works for me, may not work for you. What worked for me was practicality. Something I could easily apply to my own life.

While I can't guarantee all these tools will work for you, I can guarantee at least one of them will if you commit to it. So, play around with them. Have fun. Alter them to your liking. If I suggest ten minutes and you find that you do better with starting off at five minutes, then do that. The key is that once you find a tool, add it to your tool box, and *use* it as needed.

At first, I was reluctant to change the boys' schedules; I felt very selfish.

Looking back, I can't help but laugh. I underestimated my kids. I was so concerned about deviating from the existing structure, that I forgot their innate way of adapting to their surroundings. Within a week, the boys had their new routine down. Kids are way more resilient than we give them credit for. The adults are the ones who overthink and stress about change, not the kids.

They knew that in fifteen minutes I would come out and attend to my nightly duties with a smiling face. Within three weeks I was amazed when one evening, my youngest said to me "Mom, don't you need to go to your room for a few minutes?" (Not kidding!)

A few months down the road on the way home from school, my five year old began telling me that he had a tough day at school and asked me if he could sit quietly in my room so he could "get happier".

That was the moment I *knew* I was onto something and on the right track!

I realized I wasn't the only person benefiting. This wasn't only about me. Silently, through my actions, I was teaching the boys some essential stress tools.

We all began enjoying our time together more. I never thought weeknights could be that enjoyable and productive too. I found myself really listening to the kids more, instead of just "uh huh'ing" and "good job'ing" them to death; but truly listening with my heart.

I began to really appreciate our evening routines, the chats about school while I cooked and everything in between. I could tell the kids were really digging the "new" mom.

While this made it easy for me to keep going, we did have those days when the boys didn't want me to take a break. For those nights, I just reminded myself that they don't know what's good for me or them and proceeded as normal. I knew they'd thank me later (even if they didn't verbalize it).

So, what's the magic with my schedule?

Nothing. It's common sense really. There's nothing "airy fairy" about it. That's the beauty of it.

Here's the deal…you've got the same nightly tasks at hand, so why not do them gracefully and peacefully and allow yourself the time to reset and feel refreshed instead of blowing through them while leaving a path of destruction behind you? That was my thinking.

There was always this one thing that tried to stand in the way of my balancing act; can you guess what it was?

Me.

My own guilt.

My own motherly guilt.

All good intentions too.

So I replaced any motherly guilt with another gentle reminder that not only will my kids appreciate the "refreshed" mom, but again, I was silently giving the boys vital coping mechanisms and tools to get through life.

At the end of the day, I want my kids to be happy. Of course I would love for my boys to never have to experience pain, stress or heartache, but I know that is unrealistic. I'd much rather provide them with the essential tools in their toolbox because I know being happy doesn't mean life is going to be perfect. The tough days are just a fact of life.

At first, I'll admit, it felt counterproductive to take a moment out for myself when I had a "to-do" list that was a mile long. But, I also knew I would be so much more effective if I came back to my tasks ten minutes later feeling refreshed and rejuvenated.

Furthermore, our logical mind tells us the more work we do, the more results we produce. This is a preconceived notion that just doesn't make sense.

Taking breaks and being balanced allows us to work *smarter*, not harder.

The quality of our work improves.

Think about it.

If you're exhausted, tired, overwhelmed, and dragging your feet simply going through the motions of the task, what you're going to get back are mediocre results.

But, if you approach the task feeling refreshed and alive, you'll in fact produce spectacular results.

When I feel revitalized, I'm a better mom, a better writer, a better coach, a better speaker, and a better lover!

CHAPTER 6
Learning From Others

There have been days where I'd be running all over the place, juggling a zillion things at once, desperately trying to get everything done.

I'd look around and see my fiancé sitting quietly on his computer and my kids just chilling.

It would go through me like a knife.

My inner voice would be SCREAMING "**Jeesh, it must be nice to be able to sit and do whatever you want. I just want to sit and do what _I_ want, but I can't!**"

I would just spin and spiral into a bad mood.

Before I knew it, the resentment grew as the time passed.

Until eventually, I became so aggravated that one wrong move or word from any of them and I just about exploded.

That is, until one day I finally had enough and the coach in me began to look for a new way to look at this and maybe even come up with a new tool. (There's always a tool.)

So, now, I do four things:

1. **Awareness** - Remember what I said earlier about it always starts with awareness. So I look at the way I feel in any given moment and if I notice any negative feelings – I see them as a red flag. I then challenge my feelings and ask *"Why am I feeling this way? How could I change the way I'm looking at this?"* Again, I can't change other people, I can only change the way I choose to look at things. In order to do that though, I must be aware of how I'm perceiving something; a situation or a person.

2. **Model after them** – Yep. You read that correctly. In this particular case, I took a look at my perceivably selfish little darlings and I watched how they were doing exactly what they wanted to do. I reminded myself there was no *real* reason I "couldn't" do the same thing, I was choosing to do other things instead. When I looked at it this way, my resentment seemed foolish and I began to take responsibility for feeling this way. The only thing getting in my way of doing what I wanted to do was the belief I "should" be doing anything *but* something for myself. So ultimately, I let my family serve as a reminder that I, too, should be more "selfish".

Right then, I decided to stop what was I doing and go do something I really wanted to do; take a long hot bath. I literally left the vacuum cleaner in the middle of the living room. (I knew it'd still be there when I returned) You see, there are always things needing to be done, but rarely do we ever give ourselves the time to do the things we <u>want</u> to do. Letting the resentment build over a silly vacuum cleaner was a good waste of my energy. Especially since vacuuming wasn't an "emergency". In order to live a healthy, (mostly) balanced life, you've got to be willing to set aside the things you need to do and trade them in for something you want to do, even if only momentarily.

3. **Responsibility for my own well-being** – Here's another thing I realized when I took a step back. I can't expect *anyone* to be a mind reader. My family had no idea I needed help with the house. I was trying to do everything myself. When I returned after my bath (feeling calm and relaxed), I politely *asked* everyone in the house for some help.

Guess what happened? They stopped what they were doing and they helped me. To me, this was a much better solution than just (impatiently) waiting for them to ask me if I needed help, especially since often times I'd turn around and get mad when they didn't offer. Usually what would happen if I tried to wait for them to ask is that I'd become so aggravated and fed up that I'd just end up screaming and yelling at them. I realized just how ludicrous this was though. (No wonder men say women are complicated.) It serves us all so much better if we just <u>ask</u>.

4. *Be Present.* I recently read a study that said we have more distractions in one day than a caveman had in an entire lifetime! It's no wonder we feel exhausted by the end of the day. We have

become so connected, between social media, work emails, personal emails, texting, that we have become totally disconnected; not only from others, but from ourselves.

Going back to what I said earlier about noticing what you're noticing; when you start to pay attention to your inner chatter, you'll find that you tend to spend most of your time in the past or in the future. It's as if we wake up and hit some kind of invisible "auto-play" button in the morning and we start dwelling on all the things that have gone wrong or could go wrong. This not only takes up our precious present moment, but it produces unwanted anxiety and adds stress to our lives.

> *"If there is one thing that can eat up our present moment, its fear, doubt and worry."*

When we place our attention in the past, whether we're rehashing a conversation that ended up turning into an argument or dwelling on an opinion someone had about our outfit, we're holding ourselves in a place that no longer exists.

If I asked you to bring me a cup of your past, could you?

Impossible.

Now, don't get me wrong, I'm *sure* you could give me plenty of stories that involve your past which all may feel very real to you.

An example of this would be to imagine I asked you to recall, retell, and describe to me in great detail one of the most painful emotional experiences of your life. You would more than likely be *able* to do it. While some may not *wish* to do it because it's simply too painful.

Chances are, as you described the details of the event, you would more than likely express some of the same emotions you experienced at the time the event actually took place.

As you recall the specifics, you would undoubtedly find your body acting as though the event were taking place in the present moment. Tears may begin to flow. Angry emotions may begin to surface. Resentments may begin to build all over again. It would be as if it were happening all over again.

This is often why we turn our cheek to the most painful challenges of our lives. We avoid facing them. We shove them down with all our other crap we've accumulated.

We think if we just ignore it, the pain will go away like a dog begging for food.

Oh wait, that doesn't happen.

Exactly!

Instead, we get angry and we end up replaying the same old stories over-and-over in our heads. Our internal dialogue becomes a broken record. This happens most when our brains are doing monotonous tasks.

We *love* to hang out in the past while we're driving, walking, taking a shower, or brushing our teeth. Without even realizing it, we get ourselves all worked up, sometimes even before walking out the front door in the morning.

But *physically*, the "past" doesn't exist. The past is basically compiled of our thoughts that have been formed into memories. These memories are later formed into what we call our "beliefs".

Unfortunately, we also know the past can't be changed; it's done, finished, over.

Where the past really trips us up is when we base our present circumstances on our past experiences.

We judge and unfairly treat others based on our past.

The problem with this is that we are making assumptions based on the information we currently have on hand.

The only problem is; the way we're looking at things might be distorted.

But we can always choose to change how we *look* at the past.

Many Buddhists consider huge difficulties to be a sign of an "old soul"—the bigger the challenges and misfortunes you've experienced, the closer you are to enlightenment.

Whether you believe this or not, it's certainly uplifting to reframe all your life's bad events as tests of your character.

If you've felt particularly tested in the past (or even now) ask yourself what you're being tested for. What valuable lessons did you learn as a result of going through the things you went through?

Maybe it was patience? Compassion? Resilience? Forgiveness? Open-mindedness?

What weaknesses did you develop into strengths as a result?

When something was going wrong in my life I'd often ask "Why is this happening to me?"

One of the best things I ever did for myself was shift my mindset and replace "Why is this happening to me" to "Why is this happening for me?"

This principle can be applied to past and present.

Now let's talk about the future for a bit…

Worry McWorrysome

Now for the future; let's talk about how worry can interfere with our present moment just as much as the past can.

When you worry and/or doubt, you're essentially creating a scenario in your head that has yet to even exist. These scenarios you may muster up are filled with all the *possible* things that *could* go wrong.

As much as you love to plan your days, weeks, months and even years, there are some things that are just out of your control. It's one thing to set goals and work towards achieving them, but if you're not careful, worry can literally suck the life out of you.

When you worry, you end up skipping right past the present moment. You pass through it on the way to somewhere else, and in doing so; you miss the moment at hand.

This is how life ends up passing you by - we do it to ourselves day-in-and- day-out.

Worrying gets in the way because while you endlessly rattle off all the things you're worried about inside that little head of yours. You're also activating certain feelings in your body that make you think and believe it's happening in the present moment.

If you want to enjoy your life more, be in the moment. Be in the present moment. Not just physically, but mentally too.

Be like a baby and observe everything. Notice children at play, the clouds in the sky, the breeze on your face, the birds in flight, and the couple holding hands.

Those who say the world is ugly, fail to see the beauty that surrounds them.

We're so used to going through our day lost in our own little world; oblivious to what truly matters.

Most of you have driven down the highway/interstate, so you know there are usually three lanes to pick from.

You've got the left lane also known as the "fast lane". Then there's the middle lane. Of course all the way to the right you've got the right lane, which is also known as the "slow lane".

FAST LANE

Commuters

Those who pass

CRUISE LANE

Maintain legal speed

Cruise Control

CRUISE LANE

Below Normal Speed

I'll admit, for years I drove as though someone were chasing me in the dark. I'd hop around, switching from lane to lane, in such a hurry to get to my destination.

Nowadays, you'll see me comfortably driving in the middle lane.

The interstate can be used as a visual reminder for how to live our lives in the healthiest possible way; stay in the middle (present) lane to avoid the chaos around you.

PAST LANE

Dwelling on the same old stories

Bitterness

Inability to move forward – "stuck"

PRESENT LANE

Embracing the present no matter where you are

Maintaining balance

Trusting you'll be led

Enjoying the presence of those around you

FUTURE LANE

Worrying about tomorrow

Doubting things will work out

Fear of what lies ahead

The next time you're cruising down the interstate, let the middle lane serve as a reminder to stay in the present moment.

Staying present, means staying right where you are – no matter what you're doing – you're fully there; in the present moment.

Whether you're folding laundry or making a sandwich, be fully present. Instead of letting your thoughts just wander aimlessly all over the place, feel the t-shirt in your hands as you fold it, and pay attention to the knife that spreads your mayonnaise as you notice all the little crevices on the crust of the bread.

It sounds silly, simple and trivial, I know. But, that's just it. Simplicity is the key to living a (mostly) balanced life. You'd be amazed at what this minor adjustment can do for your well-being and mind-frame.

Two more tried and true techniques:

1) Take a breath

Breatheeeeeee. We know the two constants in life are change and the breath. Here's the thing though; the latter isn't even guaranteed. Being present and fully aware starts with the breath. Right now, right where you are, (yes right now) simply just take a big, looooong, deep breath. In through your nose and out through your mouth.

When I began paying attention to my breath, I noticed that most of the time I was holding it. I didn't allow the air to weave through my lungs and oxygenate my brain as much as I could have.

Essentially, I was depriving my body the optimal amount of oxygen it needs to *thrive*.

I noticed this especially when I was stressed. My breathing was shallow. It's no wonder I had frequent headaches throughout the day.

Once I became aware of my self-suffocation, I simply began taking a few deep breaths at random moments throughout the day. Immediately, I noticed a considerable improvement in my moods as well as an ability to handle all the things on my plate with ease and grace and my headaches subsided as an added bonus.

If you've ever birthed a child or witnessed the birth of a child, you surely remember that wonderful Lamaze breathing technique, don't you?

It's a very powerful technique. It was that very technique that allowed me to birth my two eight-pound baby boys all natural, without the use of an epidermal or drugs. (Apparently breathing gave me super-hero powers!)

2.) On a scale of 1-10, how present am I right now?

Consider asking yourself this question throughout the day to check in. Send a delayed email or reminder to yourself if you have to.

Have you ever been going about your merry way, driving down the road and a song comes over the radio and immediately you're taken back to a certain point in your life? Perhaps it reminded you of an ex or a particularly challenging point of time in your life. Maybe the memory was so painful you said "UGH, I HATE THAT SONG," and quickly changed the channel.

Here's the thing though, it wasn't the song you hate, you just hate the memories the song produces; your brain has associated that song with a painful memory.

The good news is that while you can't control the past, you can control the way you *think* about the past.

Here's an example of how a simple song on the radio can lead down an ugly path…

"What a jerk! I cannot believe he cheated on me!"

"Damn I hate men!"

"I Will Survive…"

YES! "At first I was afraid--- I was petrified…"

"He sucks so bad for ruining our lives!"

"I can't believe I was such a FOOL--never again!"

Look at what just happened in the diagram. That example was from my very own personal experience. Each thought connected to the next thought in some way. In no time at all, a simple song on the radio caused me to reminisce about all the difficulties that took place during this one particular tough time period in my life.

Those negative thoughts would continue even after the song was over. I became so angry at my ex-husband that I would react as though it were happening all over again. If I really got going, I'd even send him random nasty texts; all because a song stirred up some strong, old emotions.

To think, all because of some silly song lyrics that triggered these painful memories. These are what I call "triggers of our past". That's all they are; triggers.

Moments like these take away from our present moment. So, simply being aware of where you are in your present moment often does the trick. You can bring yourself back to the present moment at any given time.

When someone is talking to us, most of the time we are somewhere else.

We walk around living in everywhere but the present moment. While we may think we are "spending time with the family", most of the time we are mentally off in a far distant land. We spend our time in the past; dwelling, rehashing, analyzing, and maybe even seething. Then, we look to tomorrow, rattling off our list of things to do. We half-listen to our loved ones and sometimes don't even listen at all, because we are consumed with—-the past, the future, social media emails, and texting.

Our kids tell us meaningful stories about their day, and with our body language we silently convey the message that we don't care (even though we truly do).

Then, we wonder why the kids of today have no idea how to communicate, engage in a conversation, tell their parents what's going on in their lives, or share their feelings.

Kids, whether old and young, need to feel heard by their parents. In fact, we all want to be heard. Adults are no exception.

I ask you; "Are you listening to those around you – are you really listening?"

Staying in the present moment takes practice. There are bills to pay, meetings at work, kids to pick up, a house to clean, doctor's appointments, shows to watch, parents to please, loved ones to miss, and the list goes on-and-on. With all that going on - past *and* future - it's no wonder that presence is so hard to pin down. It isn't, however, as hard as you might believe.

As with learning any new skill, you've got to start somewhere, right?

You'll notice, especially at first, that your mind wanders a lot. That's okay, though. Once you're aware, you can shift it to a thought that serves you better.

When I first started out, these little tools worked really well to help bring me back to the present moment...

- Rather than simply racing through traffic, I drove down the road feeling my hands on the steering wheel and feeling the wheel's grooves on my fingertips.
- I began noticing the birds near my car and the trees blowing in the wind when I stopped at a red light.
- I noticed the people in the car sitting next to me and I noticed the expression on their faces.
- I took take a big deep breath and imagined myself fogging up a mirror in front of my nose.
- While in the shower, I began noticing the water hitting my back, the way my fingers and scalp felt as I massaged the shampoo into my hair rather than rattling off my "to-do" list.
- As I folded laundry, I focused on folding laundry. I felt the cloth in between my hands and I didn't let the other items on my "to-do" list consume me.
- When it came to my kids, I realized that fifteen minutes of my undivided attention was more valuable than an hour of my multi-tasking with my phone or laptop in front of my face. I noticed the more present I was, the more fulfilled they felt and the better I felt too.

CHAPTER 7
Seeing Yourself through the Eyes of Others

MIRROR-MIRROR ON THE WALL...

Giving up my heart took every ounce of my being when it came to my dating life. I really had to push myself to open my heart. Often, I failed epically. I spent *years* protecting myself and building my walls. I'd try to tell myself (and others) that every guy I dated started with a "brand new fresh slate".

Although I even believed this myself, that was bullshit. Total bullshit.

I looked for things. I interrogated without appearing I was interrogating. I mentally took notes of every answer, logging them for later use. I was like one of those sniffer dogs, trained to sniff out the things that just didn't add up. I was ready to find something wrong, anything. The more I liked the guy, the more skeptical I was, and the more I questioned. Of course, I would never reveal any of this to him. On the outside, it appeared as though I wasn't giving this guy any thought. I was calm, cool and collected and apparently, guys loved that. The more I backed away, the closer they wanted to get....the closer they wanted to get, the more I backed away.

Funny how that works, isn't it?

I mastered the game. Only, I wasn't playing a game, I was just numb. I believed less-and-less in the "happily ever after".

When I'd meet a nice guy, I'd blow them off because *"If it seemed too good to be true, it probably was"*.

Here's the funny thing, (well, not really). Even with all this, I had thoroughly convinced myself that I could maintain a relationship this way.

Boy, was I mistaken!

It wasn't until years later (and many "frogs" later) that I met a very special someone (my now fiancé). He made me truly want to open my heart.

He came into my life when I least expected it too. At a time I was closed off to love (or so I thought).

I had just ended a one-year relationship. I always had this self-imposed rule of not dating anyone any sooner than at least ninety days after a break-up. Often times, I'd give myself six months or more to heal and enjoy time by myself.

I remember soon after my breakup, my best friend and I were working late at the office one evening, having one of those total girl conversations.

"I am "DONE" with men!" I declared.

"Whatever! You are not done with men. You just need to get out there! Go casually date a bunch of guys and have fun!" She suggested.

"You know what.... I'm just gonna' date a bunch of guys and play them like little fools, break their hearts and cheat on them just like they've all done to me! I am so sick of being the "good-girl".

(I was just a tad bitter.)

It wasn't my style to casually date several guys at once. It seemed like that took way too much effort and energy. Both of which I didn't have the time for.

I just need to find someone who's light and fluffy; who expects nothing in return. Not a one night stand, but just fun." I told her.

And then...

Life brought me Josh.

He was planning to move to California in just a few short months, he was four years younger than I was, never married and he had no kids.

Score.

Well, needless to say he didn't end up moving. And here we are six years later and stronger than ever.

{You really just never know.}

One of the toughest things I had to face early on in our relationship was just how much the barriers around my heart got in the way of my ability to let love in.

Josh made my heart grow in ways I never thought possible. My journey with him forced me to look within.

I wanted to be a "tough girl" forever, but I knew if I wanted a healthy, long-lasting relationship, I would have to at least *try* to forgive and shed my past.

The love I had in my heart for Josh scared me. Actually, it **petrified** me.

I tried ignoring it, but it couldn't be denied. I even tried to fight it.

He saw right through my "tough-girl attitude" and he had no problems calling me out on it either.

One day about a year into our relationship, we were having an argument in the parking lot of his office after work one night. I don't even remember what we were arguing about, but I vividly remember him leaning into my car, listening to me go on about this and that.

At one point, I said to him *"We just need to break up, I need to stop listening to my heart and listen with my head for once in my life!"*

He disputed *"That's just it Jody! That's you're problem. You're too busy listening with that head of yours and not listening to your heart enough!"*

{Ouch}

I was irate! So irate that I sped off and left him standing there. It was one of those movie moments, where I looked in my rear view mirror and saw him standing there alone.

As I drove down the road, a flood of emotions washed over me. In the midst of my anger though, I softened.

His words rang through me.

I explored them deeply. In that instant, I knew there was a great deal of truth. They ran deep and stuck with me.

In heart of hearts I didn't want to break-up. I was just scared and up until this point in my life it was always easier to run.

I knew I had to do the very thing I committed to *never* doing again.

I had to learn (force myself really) how to truly open my heart and let love in again.

That was one of the most difficult things I've ever done; open to love like I had never done before. My baggage was getting heavy and I was so tired of carrying it around.

I was ready to set it down, but this meant I had to push myself beyond my comfort zone and into the land of the unknown.

Even though falling in love, letting my guard down and becoming vulnerable again scared the pants off me...I knew it was something that had to be done.

Not for him, not even for us, but for me.

I had no idea how I would do it. All I knew at this point was that I'd commit to it and stumble my way through it anyway.

The tool I'm about to give you is one of the first ones I started with.

It's a tool my clients now rely on too.

It will provide you with an opportunity to really look in the mirror and *see* beyond the surface.

Ultimately, the tool will allow you to grow and evolve into the person you're meant to become.

I'll let you know now though, it will also require you to take a closer look at those "ugly" parts of yourself, too.

You know, the ones you've tried to shove down and hide from the outside world.

Yep, those.

You may find your knee-jerk reaction is to turn your cheek to those parts, but don't. Just embrace them because the beauty of the "ugly" parts is that they are in fact what hold the key.

This tool will only work for those who are able to take a step back and really take a good look inside.

The effectiveness of this tool is dependent upon the level of honesty and openness of the person.

You may not like what you see. But, with practice and self-forgiveness, you'll find this principle to be the easiest to apply and the most transformational when it comes to relationships.

The Looking Glass

What if I told you that the world around you acted as a mirror; in every moment, in every situation and in every relationship?

I'm sure you've heard the saying "You treat people how you want them to treat you". Well, let's peel back the layers and dive in deeper....

Within every challenge is an opportunity to learn something about ourselves. When you take the time to self-reflect, you ultimately learn something about yourself. Essentially, that's how we grow.

Growth is a good thing. Actually, it's an *A-mazing* thing, its food for the soul.

When we apply this "looking glass" principle specifically to our relationships and the people within them, we become aware of all the things *we* too need to work on.

My mom has a mirror on her bathroom counter; it's one of those magnified ones. She loves it, it's great for plucking your eyebrows, and *"it shows <u>everything</u>,"* she says.

I think it's both disgusting and addicting. I could sit there for hours just picking away at those tiny little specks on my face. Gross.

The mirror *is* very revealing, to say the least. Mom's right, you can see *everything*!

Well, we're about to look at *that* kind of mirror. One designed to magnify , only, this mirror is designed to see on the *inside*.

Before we do that, however, there are a just a couple more reminders when applying this principle:

1. You must be willing to step back and view your life from afar. Imagine your life is a "sitcom" and you're in your living room watching yourself on the TV screen in front of you. You're not judging, you're just watching the scenes. Simply notice.

2. Once you see the "ugly" parts of yourself (and you will), you have to be easy on yourself. Refrain from condemning yourself or feeling ashamed. Your main goal is to simply accept it as knowledge.

3. Once you've identified the parts of yourself you dislike, you've got to be willing to take action and adjust your ways to more loving ones. This won't happen overnight, so just be patient.

Let's Get To It...

"Relationships are a perfect mirror of your inner relationship with yourself."

The people in your life and relationships, even the most difficult ones, are merely reflecting parts of your own consciousness back to you.

Translation: Relationships are a perfect mirror of your *inner* relationship with yourself.

The beliefs you've acquired about life and love have a way of showing up in our *external* relationships. The perception of ourselves shows up in the people we surround ourselves with.

In order for you to recognize a certain quality in another, it must be part of your consciousness/awareness. You couldn't see it otherwise.

That's why you were attracted to the friends you've picked, as well as your lovers. You noticed a quality that agreed with yours and you formed a relationship to varying degrees because of it. You were "attracted" to this person (and their qualities) in one way or another.

Everything you admire in another person belongs to *you* as well. Every quality that you see in your partner, whether you admire it or not, is your mirror –

It is showing you *who* you are.

That's the easy part.

Here's where it can get tricky…

What about the difficult people in my life? Does this mean I have similar qualities and I was "attracted" to them, also?

Yep.

So what I'm saying is that I was attracted to their negative qualities, too?

Yep.

{Bear with me….}

When someone gets under our skin and rubs us the wrong way, we are so quick to point fingers at them and place blame. Often, *we* feel victimized.

When we apply the "looking glass" tool to the challenging people in our lives, we'll find they too are mirroring back to us the personality traits we have within *ourselves*; the good, the bad, and the ugly.

The reason we feel negatively towards a person and/or their actions is because they are reflecting a certain aspect of ourselves that we've *refused* to look at; the parts of ourselves that we've tried to shove down and ignore.

When we notice the flaws in others and attempt to condemn them, we are only irritated because deep down, we know that we're not addressing the very same issues within ourselves.

{Gulp}

Essentially, the deeper cause of break-ups and divorce happens when one or both partners can no longer stand to see themselves in the other person.

Every single person in your life is your mirror.

Look back at your past (and present) relationships. Do you find they are very similar? Can you see a pattern? Are you attracted to people with similar qualities? People with the same problems, but with different faces?

We are truly creatures of habit, so when you look at all your relationships, even the non-romantic ones, you'll more than likely see a pattern of some sort.

Relationship patterns are inevitable. The real question is, do you like the pattern you see? Have they served you? Are they bringing out the best in you, or are they bringing out the worst?

When I began applying this principle to my own relationships, I noticed how I was always facing the same problems, I had the same feelings and even the same insecurities, and they continued to repeat themselves over-and-over. I definitely had a pattern.

For a while, I thought the cause of my heartbreak was because I was dating the "wrong guys".

When I really took a step back, the ugly truth was that there was one common denominator.

Me.

{Crap}.

Boy was that realization a wakeup call for me. More like a rude awakening, because this whole time I was thinking it was *"them"* who had the problem.

Really, *I* was the "problem".

Ouch.

As much as it hurt to acknowledge this, it was a vital piece of my growth.

For years, I surrendered to the belief that relationships were difficult and they required so much compromise and effort. This made it easy for me to lose hope and give up when it came to love.

I've said to my friends many times before *"I'm never dating again!"* and *"I'm never getting married again!"*

I'd often wondered things like *"Why do I always fall for the unavailable guys?"* or *"Why am I the one who's only attracted to the jerks, the assholes and the ones who run from commitment?"* Or *how about this one, "Why can't I just fall for the guys who are nice, loving, honest and sweet?"* What is wrong with me?"

No matter how many times I tried to change someone or even tried to change the face of the person sitting next to me, the fundamentals of my relationship seemed to always remain *unchanged*.

This was because they were simply *mirroring* me.

The reflection I was "seeing" was the inner relationship I had with <u>*myself*</u>.

At the time, I was distant, guarded, and silently screaming *"get the hell away from me—-I don't want to get hurt again!"*

I silently pushed them away.

So, my external relationships showed themselves the very same way. They showed me who I was. Or, who I <u>*thought*</u> I was. They showed me parts of myself that I was refusing to acknowledge. It was no wonder I repelled the guys who were truly ready for a commitment.

Now, let's take a peek at *your* mirror....

Interestingly, the more you dislike a certain quality in someone, the more it is showing you a part of yourself that you're not acknowledging.

Here are a few examples:

- Do you get aggravated when those around you are competitive? Look inside, where in your life are you too competitive? Relationships? Health? Career? Finances?
- Do you often feel your partner or those around you aren't listening to you? Do you frequently feel unheard? Look in the mirror, who are *you* not truly hearing? Do you often "uh-huh" your kids to death? Maybe it's towards your spouse, co-worker, boss, or parent.
- Does it drive you nuts when someone tries to "control you"? Where in your life are you yourself controlling? Do you have to have the laundry done a certain way? Are you constantly micromanaging your kids, or spouse? What areas could you back off a bit?
- If you're partner's jealous behaviors irritates you, it's likely that, somewhere there's a jealousy streak in you too. Maybe specifically to your partner, but it can be of others too—-maybe a co-worker or a friend.
- Do you hate always feeling like you're being criticized by someone? Never quite feeling you "measure up"? Where in your

life are you overly critical? It could be that you're overly critical to your children, co-workers, friends or other family members. It could also be that you're too critical of yourself.

- How about the negativity or insecurities of others? Does that get under your skin? Dig deep and you may find that you too, have a negative nature and similar insecurities in some area of your life.

The only reason that any of these qualities are annoying you is because they also belong to you; and they will *continue* to reflect and aggravate you for as long as you continue to ignore them as your *own*.

These annoyances are appearing in your life to *teach* you something about *yourself*. Once you own up to them, it gives you a chance to re-discover and ultimately, re-define yourself.

This allows you to grow into the amazing person you truly are.

Essentially, you teach others how to treat you by how you treat *yourself*. You have to love yourself and truly feel deserving of a loving, healthy relationship.

This "looking glass" principle works well with everybody; family, friends, co-workers, bosses, the cashier, and anybody else you interact with throughout your day.

Please note: Everyone is on their own path. It doesn't always have to do with you. Remember that their actions are independent of you and coming from a place of who _they_ are. Unknowingly, people often project their own fears, doubts and worries onto others.

CHAPTER 8
Forgiveness

Whether we're forgiving another person or ourselves, forgiveness is a huge piece of getting from point A to point B and improving our lives.

"Forgiveness is the art of self-love."

It's all a part of building our home on a healthy foundation.

It's nearly impossible to move forward if there is still forgiveness to be done.

The more pain, heartbreak, and sorrow you've experienced in your life, the more you need to forgive.

In fact, everybody on this planet needs to forgive.

When you consciously *try* to forgive, you end up living a more peaceful life. That is what most strive for; inner peace. Inner peace is true freedom.

Trying to move forward with your life without forgiving is like trying to run through a big pile of mud…with flip-flops on.

It doesn't matter how fast you run, what type of shape you're in, how old you are, how many college degrees or certifications you have, what books you've read or what seminars you've attended; the fastest runner in the world would get stuck in mud and literally come to a halt.

If it were to rain however, that mud would become diluted with water and it would be an entirely different story....you'd be able to move through it much easier.

It's the same with forgiveness. If we dilute those resentments and regrets with love and compassion, the pain will be dissolved by forgiveness, and as a result, our hearts will open and we can move forward freely.

Forgiveness essentially removes the blocks that get in the way of love.

So, its imperative you figure out how to forgive. But, keep in mind, forgiveness is a process; sometimes a daily one.

Forgiving Others:

To forgive in the moments when we're betrayed by someone we deeply love and trust, your soul is influenced in a very powerful way.

Common Misconceptions

Often times, I hear that a person's unwillingness to forgive has to do with their misbelief that forgiveness has to do with the *other* person and *nothing* to do with us.

If we take a closer look at this misbelief, we'll find that it's quite the opposite.

Forgiveness has absolutely NOTHING to do with the other person and *everything* to do with US.

Forgiveness releases the death grip of energy it has on <u>you</u>. Let's face it, it takes a great deal of energy to hold onto resentments. When you forgive, you're essentially releasing the energy that has a hold on you.

Another common misbelief I hear most often is that forgiveness is "impossible" because it means the person "will get away with something."

For years, I believed this too.

They're both completely inaccurate though.

Forgiving a person does not mean you allow *anyone* to walk all over you or that you deny the other person's responsibility for hurting you. It most certainly doesn't mean that you minimize or justify the wrong doing either.

> *"You can forgive a person without excusing the act."*

You *can* forgive a person without excusing the act.

Forgiving another person doesn't create a relationship either. Last time I checked, relationships were based on a *mutual* benefit.

Right?

The bottom line is that forgiveness brings inner peace. It allows you to move on with your life. Forgiving someone isn't going to happen overnight, but you've got to start somewhere.

Where do you start?

Forgiveness begins with compassion.

For years, I truly believed I forgave my dad for his suicide. I didn't even realize I was holding on as much as I was. I guess it was because I was standing too close to my own picture. I was caught up in me-me-me and how the loss affected *my* life. While I considered myself a suicide "survivor", in my mind, I was also a suicide victim.

Once I was finally able to take a step back and view my dad's suicide walking in *his* shoes, forgiveness evolved. I became compassionate for *his* story. It was no longer, *my* story. It was no longer about me.

Through compassion, I was finally able to understand that his suicide had *nothing* to do with me.

I began to really understand things from where *he* was standing.

For years, I searched endlessly for the answers to that one burning question "*Why* did he do it?"

Without a suicide note, I was left to fill in the blanks on my own. I just wanted answers. I *needed* answers and so desperately needed closure. Day in and day out, for all the years after his suicide, that question burned in my mind.

It haunted me.

What I found interesting was through compassion, the "why" became less-and-less important to me. Figuring out the "why" wasn't going to do me any good or change the fact that my dad had taken his life. This was a hard truth I finally accepted, and it ultimately opened the doors to truly forgiving my dad once and for all.

This allowed me to move forward in my life.

Of course, these realizations wouldn't bring my dad back or change the outcome either. The hard truth was that my dad was gone and there was nothing I could do about that.

I, on the other hand, was in fact still living and breathing. I knew I had a choice to make. I could either go on living in the past or forgive him.

When I forgave him, it released *me*. It not only released me from my own victim-hood, but it released me from my past, present, *and* future.

I realized I was repeating the same patterns my dad had. Like him, I was using my present moment to fill it with the "what-if's" and all the "shoulda's, coulda's, and woulda's."

Most of the time, a person doesn't wake up one day and just decide to take their life. Suicide starts with an internal dialogue the person is having with themselves; a dialogue about life that often goes on for years. Eventually, this internal dialog (and many other factors) leads to their suicide.

My dad held onto his pain, the regrets, the resentments of his life, and I was heading down that very same road.

People who die by suicide don't really want to end their life; they just want to end their *pain.*

So, in my darkest moments, while I may have chosen *not* to take my own life and continue "living", I was really only living a half lived life.

My inability to forgive my dad prevented me from truly living life to the fullest. In many ways, I was paralyzed by the pain that surrounded his death. At the end of the day though, I knew my dad would not want this for me.

When I finally saw things through new lenses, I was able to forgive my dad and regain my power.

When we have compassion for a person or their situation, we understand there is a *bigger* picture. And, like I've said before, the most challenging people in our lives are the most influential.

They can help us become better people. But, only if we allow it and we learn to forgive. This is the gift of forgiveness. And, it truly is an amazing gift!

"Let forgiveness be the substitute for fear. This is the only rule for happy dreams." ~ A Course In Miracles

The Difficult People in Your Life

A big part of my soul-searching frenzy to clean up my life required me to look at my past and all the people in it and ask myself *"Where is there forgiveness work yet to be done?"*

Like most ex-husbands, mine challenged me.

I knew I had a great deal of forgiving to do when it came to him.

I spent many years after our divorce resenting him for all the things he did while we were married; for destroying our home and the chance of our happy ever-after. I despised him for adopting my oldest son only to cheat on me while I was pregnant with my second. I hated him for all the new challenges our divorce brought. I didn't want to be a single mom with two kids. I blamed him for my new financial struggles. I felt foolish for ever believing in the happy-ever-after. I was bitter that I let my guard down for him in the first place. I often looked at him in disgust.

Several years after our divorce, my ex-husband and I were going through court proceedings once again. Only this time, Josh and I were attempting to relocate to a larger city to follow the opportunities presented to us.

There was one problem though; in the state of Florida in order to relocate with my boys, I had to get my ex-husband to agree. Needless to say, he wasn't pleased with our wanting to move and he wasn't about to make it easy for us.

Boy, did he test me. It would have been very easy for me to get caught up in that vicious web of tit- for-tat childish behaviors.

Thank goodness I had the tools to cope this time. I knew while I couldn't control *his* actions, I could control my *re*actions to his behavior.

During the course of the twelve months our proceedings took place, he presented me with ample opportunities to practice this whole compassion and forgiveness thing.

When he did something to really tick me off and I felt the sudden desire to stab him in the eye with a dull pencil, instead, I just stopped. I took a few deep breaths, and I did whatever it took for me to calm myself down and re-center myself. Sometimes, I'd scream into a pillow. Other times, I'd just go out for a power-walk to blow off some steam.

I knew I had to release my negative energy; otherwise it would wind up consuming me. I knew it didn't do me any good to hold it all inside. I also knew lashing out on him wouldn't help me either.

In those heated moments, where he was _**really**_ testing me…once I got to a point where I could actually think straight again, I'd mentally wish him well and forgive him.

It helped to remind myself that he was acting like a scared little child. When I took a step back and saw things from _his_ prospective, I realized he was fearful of not seeing his children as much as he wanted to.

I could see that he felt as though he was "losing" them in a way.

Could I really blame him for that?

Not really.

Regardless of our past, he loved his children dearly.

If the shoe was on the other foot, I'd be scared too.

Once I realized this, I was able to have compassion for _his_ story.

Now, this didn't mean I allowed him to talk to me or treat me in a disrespectful manner. What it meant was that I was taking personal responsibility for my _own_ well-being.

I knew it did MY well-being no good to yell and scream back at him. This would only feed into his already overflowing negative energy.

Instead, I would just quietly hang up the phone and refuse to answer it again until I knew he calmed down. Or, as much as I wanted to text him back, I refrained.

I did this for *me*, not for *him*.

I was finally able to see that beyond his actions, there was an opportunity for me to grow. I actually learned to not take it personally.

He was just another *vehicle* for me to learn these fundamental lessons my soul clearly still needed to learn. This shift in perception allowed me to actually become grateful for all that he was bringing out in me.

He forced me to grow. He *pushed* me.

I began referring to him as a "weed". Ya' know, those annoying little buggers that just keep popping up. No matter what you do to try to get rid of them, they always seem to come back to annoy you.

Well, this "weed" was popping up because it needed to be handled once and for all.

I wanted nothing more than to move forward and start a new life in another city and I knew in order to do that, I had to face this "weed" in the most loving, healing way possible.

I am glad to report that nowadays, we've both healed from the past and we have a great relationship. But we had to go through some ugly times in order to get to where we are today. We have both grown a great deal.

If you're feeling particularly challenged by a "special someone" right now, ask yourself a few questions:

- What am I being tested for?
- Instead of asking "Why is this happening to me", try asking "Why is this happening for me?
- What strengths must I develop further? Patience, compassion, forgiveness?

You must commit to stop letting the past continue to haunt the present moment because it also affects your future.

Forgiving Yourself

Although forgiving ourselves can actually be even harder than forgiving someone else, it *is* possible.

When we're carrying around a sense of blame for something that has happened in the past, this can lead us to a never-ending, inescapable sense of unhappiness.

It can also wreak havoc on our mind, spirit and body.

As a matter of fact, numerous studies have shown those who experience high levels of anger are more prone to heart disease and illness.

(Kam, 2014) Jerry Kiffer, MA, a heart-brain researcher at the Cleveland Clinic's Psychological Testing Center states "It causes wear and tear on the heart and cardiovascular system."

> *"Forgiving yourself releases you from the past and allows you to physically and emotionally move forward; as wll as protect your general well-being."*

(Kam, 2014) According to an analysis of findings from 44 studies published in the 2013 *Journal of the American College of Cardiology*, evidence supports the link between emotions and heart disease.

Forgiving yourself releases you from the past and allows you to physically and emotionally move forward; as well as protect your general well-being.

The basics:

1. **Understanding the importance of forgiveness** – Living constantly in a state of non-forgiveness requires a great deal of energy. Our fear of being vulnerable, our burning anger and our

constant state of sadness, hurt and blame chews us up inside. Rather than dwelling on the past forgiving allows us to stay in the present moment. We can freely move forward to a future that's focused on purpose and improvement, rather than being held back by past hurts.

2. **Re-shifting your focus** - Rather than thinking about what you'll lose, shift your eyes to all that you'll *gain* when you choose to forgive.

3. **Self-Acceptance** – Don't ever feel you need to forgive yourself for being yourself. Forgiving yourself is all about targeting those things you feel bad about, not about the person you truly are. Acknowledge that you're a good person, imperfections and all. This doesn't mean you ignore the faults. It just means that above all else, you value yourself and you continue to grow as a person. Learn from what you've done, but value your whole-self. That larger part of you.

4. **Own your emotions** - Part of our struggle to forgive, simply lies in the fact that we are unable to accept the emotions we are experiencing: fear, anger, resentment, and vulnerability. So, instead of trying to shove down your feelings in an attempt to avoid them, be willing to accept them as they come. Once a problem is identified, it can be handled and later dissolved.

5. **Perfectionism** - This one is a real gem; a vicious cycle. Perfectionism forces us to hold ourselves to a higher standard;

one that we wouldn't even hold anyone else to. {Guilty as charged.} The vicious cycle starts when we're way too hard on ourselves. But, when we welcome our own imperfections, it allows us to accept that all human beings are imperfect. Every living soul. Embrace your imperfections.

6. **Release the expectations of others** – Never feeling good enough can leave you feeling stuck. Self-forgiveness is essential. The truth is you really have no control of what other people do or say. People say things and treat others based on their own stories and often times they're dealing with their own "demons". Forgive yourself for trying to live a life according to their expectations. Begin making changes according to your own rules. For everyone who has ever been hard on you keep in mind there was once someone in their life who was hard on them. Be kind to yourself. Strive to be the best you can be and release the need to please others.

7. **Banishing Self-Punishment** – Earlier I mentioned that forgiving another can be difficult because often we feel it "condones" their behavior. Of course we know now this is not true. Apply the same principle to yourself. You can say *"I'm not proud of what I've done, but I'm moving on for the sake of my health, my well-being, and those around me."*

8. **Forgiveness is a journey, not a destination** – Of course you've heard this before. It helps to take the pressure off when

we understand that forgiveness is a process and it takes practice, self-love, commitment, understanding, and patience. You will have ups-and-downs and you'll never do it perfectly. But again, perfection isn't the goal; moving forward is. So, when you find yourself beating yourself up for forgiving one day and going back to "square one" the next, just let the slip-up be an indicator that you still have forgiving to do. Again, nobody is telling you that you must forgive within a certain amount of time; we place those unrealistic expectations on ourselves.

CHAPTER 9
Overcoming Fear

Besides just a four-letter F word, what is fear?

FEAR is simply RESISTANCE. You can resist many things, such as love, success, and change.

Does fear truly exist, though? Can you bring me jar of your fear?

If we know our thoughts are based on past experiences and how we interpret the experience at hand (also known as our perception), then we also know our perception isn't only about "facts".

Here's the thing I've come to know about perception - it becomes fogged by our pain, our sorrow, our unwillingness to forgive, the resentments we hold towards others, and the ugly regrets of our past. (And everything else in between.)

What ultimately ends up happening is that our view becomes extremely distorted.

Just the same way a person wears "rose-colored glasses"; we can put on our "doom n' gloom-colored glasses", too. The way we look at the world around us and the people in it can become ugly when we've been hurt, betrayed, and disappointed.

We can find ourselves no longer trusting others as easily as we once did; holding back and not giving ourselves fully to another. We're reluctant to open our hearts, we negatively analyze the intentions of others, and we become cynical, judgmental, and sarcastic.

Our trust in overall humanity, love, and the idea of "happily-ever after" can quickly fade away.

We've got to be willing to challenge how we *interpret* our experiences, especially our most challenging times. It's only then we can learn to re-frame them.

I call it "flipping the script".

In other words, you have to be willing to see even your most traumatic experiences in life in a new light, with new eyes, and with a fresh perspective.

You have to be able to take a step back and try with all your heart and soul to see the *good* in any circumstance.

This takes practice (and patience).

Accepting and understanding there is a bigger picture and although the challenge(s) before you may *appear* to be about you, that's not always the case.

When you were a child, did your mom or dad ever tell you not to sit too close to the T.V. because "you'll hurt your eyes"?

Imagine you're that child sitting close to the T.V., only you're not watching Saturday morning cartoons, you're watching your own life on the big screen.

Be willing to have courage and take a step back so you can view things from a new perspective.

If we peel back the layers behind our troubles, problems and difficult circumstances, we'll see a wide array of emotions, such as anger, sadness, confusion, resentment, jealousy, envy, and maybe even hatred.

> *"Fear is simply your resistance to move forward."*

But, what usually sits behind all those negative emotions is one thing that defines them all.

Fear.

Fear is simply your resistance to move forward. That's all it is.

In one of my favorite books is by Spencer Johnson, "Who Moved My Cheese?" , an insightful parable about dealing with fear and change, the author reflects on the character's recent actions:

*"He had to admit that the biggest inhibitor to change lies within yourself, and that nothing gets better until **you** change. Perhaps most importantly, he realized that there is always new cheese (a metaphor for the things you want) out there whether you recognize it at the*

time, or not. And that you are rewarded with it when you go past your fear and enjoy the adventure."

It's an incredible story, my boys even loved it. (It's a super easy read too.)

Ultimately, we have fears because we don't believe in ourselves. For whatever reason, we don't believe that we'll get through what's at hand.

To top it off, our fears cause us to worry.

We fill our heads with all sorts of worries; our finances, our kids, health, deaths, and even car accidents that haven't happened yet.

Here's the crazy thing about fear though…it's all in our heads.

If only we knew we had everything we need within us. Instead of knowing and trusting in ourselves, we allow our fears to keep us stuck and miserable.

Fear is like our bully.

"An aggressive person who intimidates or mistreats weaker people."

Nobody likes a bully.

What's the best thing to do when facing a bully?

Sure, you can turn your back, but this will only give the bully the power it's seeking.

108

The only real choice you have is to look the bully square in the eyes, face them and stand up for yourself.

According to Webster's dictionary, the definition of fear is; *an unpleasant emotion caused by the belief that someone or something is dangerous, likely to cause pain, or a threat.*

Notice the definition used the term *"belief"*. Note that it didn't use the word "fact".

In essence, fear is just a belief.

What's a belief?

It's just a thought that we think a lot. A story we tell ourselves time and time again.

Essentially, many of our fears come from our crazy belief system.

This belief system is compiled with our thoughts, feelings, interpretations, and our early programming.

But again, these interpretations are often fogged and distorted because of the pain we've experienced in the past.

So, what we're seeing isn't even accurate.

Have you ever smeared your car window with olive oil and then tried driving down the road?

{Please say no!}

So, when it comes to relationships…why in the world would we enter a relationship expecting a healthy, long-lasting, loving relationship, when the window to our heart is smeared with olive oil (the stuff of the past)?

In order to see things clearly, we have to clean our windows first.

It's only *then* we can experience a long-lasting healthy relationship or marriage.

Another key point to remember about fear is that it comes from the personality side of us. You know that smaller part of you we talked about earlier. It's that small voice that just wants to keep you small and in your comfort zone.

However, the most important thing to know about fear is this: we will *always* have fear.

I can't stand when I read motivational quotes that read: *"Be fearless."*

Its crap.

You will have fear for the rest of your life.

Fear is a survival mechanism that is useful in certain circumstances and can save our life when needed; the fight-or-flight response.

It's a basic human emotion and it will always be a part of your personality. There isn't a soul on earth that hasn't experienced fear.

There is however, a difference in how you treat fear.

The most happy and even the most successful people on earth aren't without fear.

The difference lies in what they chose to do with their fear.

For them, they pushed forward *despite* their fears while the others haven't.

They choose deliberately to kick their fears out of the driver's seat.

There's a big difference in fear having you and you having fear.

There are an endless amount of things to be fearful of.

Every person has experienced some degree of fear at one time or another in their life.

Here are 20 of the most common fears:

1. Public speaking
2. Intimacy
3. Hurting someone's feelings
4. Failure
5. Rejection
6. Not doing/being enough
7. Commitment
8. Losing a job
9. Letting our kids down

10. Letting our partners down

11. Letting our family down

12. Objects, animals

13. Getting hurt (again)

14. Losing a child

15. Losing a loved one through death

16. Losing a partner through divorce/break-up

17. Being vulnerable

18. Being less than, when compared to others

19. Success

20. Not meeting our own expectations

If we take a closer look at this list, we'll see that behind each of them, is one of two things:

1. A fear of change

2. A foggy belief system

So, let's try to clean these up.

We now know the only way we can do this is to stare them right in the eyes and face them head-on. You don't want to suppress them, you've probably already done that for years, and more than likely it's not working out that great for you.

You don't want to give these fears any more power than you've already given them. Otherwise, you'll just keep doing the same thing over-and-over and allow your life to be run by your fears.

It's not until you take personal inventory of your fears that you can take action and do something about them.

Remember, the point is never to get *rid* of your fears; the point is to learn how to work with them.

When things like death or the loss of a job happen, most of the time we have no control over them.

However, there are those times when we do have control over our circumstances.

So, whether it's the fear of moving on after a death or the fear of starting a new job, the fear of change is one of the most all-encompassing fears.

Let's take a more intimate look at a few of the fears that contain a foggy belief system.

1. **Fear of Losing a Job** - What if you looked at it as though you were being guided and the pieces we're being moved around FOR you? What if you had to lose that job in order to get a better one? Would you be so scared then?

2. **Fear of Not Doing Enough** - According to whom? An outside source? That's another endless battle that you'll never live up to.

3. **Fear of Not Being Enough** - Again, according to whom? Whose standards are you trying to live up to?

4. Fear of Letting Our Kids Down - Most parents let their kids down at some point or another. It's just a fact of life. Disappointments are a vital piece of their growth; they too have to learn their own lessons on their own path.

5. Fear of Letting Our Partners Down - Again, who doesn't let their partners down? It's a fact of life and our only goal is to be the best that we can, not for anybody else, but for ourselves.

6. Fear of Letting Our Families Down - Same thing here. Are you beginning to see the pattern here? Let go of the guilt. Just be who you truly are and don't try to be everything to everybody around you. So what if your family doesn't understand or approve of some of your decisions? You can't live for anybody else; trying to please every Tom, Dick and Harry only depletes *your* energy. The only energy that should be of any importance to you, is your own.

"We've got to feel before we can heal."

7. Fear of Getting Hurt Again - Being hurt by another is painful, especially when we've opened our hearts and trusted and believed in a person. It doesn't matter if it was a friend, a lover or a relative, it hurts and we would never want to deny or suppress the pain we feel. **We've got to feel before we can heal.** We have to allow ourselves to feel the pain and get to a point where it doesn't sting so much. Which means you take your life day-by-day, moment-by-moment and you stay in the forgiveness process. In the midst of your pain, you remind yourself that you WILL get through it, just like you got through everything else you doubted you could ever get through. As much as you need to, you remind yourself *"Everything's going to be ok. I will make it through this"*.

8. **Fear of Being Open and Vulnerable with Others** -This fear is a biggie. While on the outside we might appear to be tough, strong and confident, on the inside we may find ourselves holding back a piece of ourselves. We do this for various reasons, but the most common is because we're scared that if anybody got too close, they would see right through us. And then, they'll find out who we "really are". Allowing others to see our imperfections, insecurities and our flaws can be frightening. Perhaps what we're most afraid of is that they might see we're actually really sensitive and our feelings get hurt fairly easily and then they'll realize that we're not perfect—— OH NO! WHAT THEN?! Here's what then...they'll see that you're human and you'll see that they have the same fears. We all do, actually.

9. **Fear of Success-** This one is a sneaky little booger. Sometimes, this one is a bit harder to recognize also. This was actually one of my greatest fears. When I first started my coaching and speaking practice my greatest fear was the fear of **success**. Sounds crazy right? That fear got in the way of growing my business to the level it was capable of becoming.

Because, if you're fearful of being successful, then you'll hold back just the same as you would when you're fearful of being vulnerable. I was getting in the way of my own success because I had this underlying belief that if I was "too successful", it would mean I had to sacrifice my family time and my time spent with Josh. I felt as though I somehow had to "choose" between my family and my career; which is ludicrous. It doesn't have to be one or the other. Once I recognized this and got out of my own head, all it took was a simple shift in my perception. I began to challenge my fear of success and I started asking myself things like *"What if I didn't have to sacrifice my family time? What if it didn't have to be that way? Where am I getting this belief from? When did this start? What if my kids knew that I loved them and although maybe our family time may look a bit different, I wouldn't have to essentially choose one or the other?"* All it really took was for me to be open to the change and look for new ways to incorporate our family time. While it may have required me/us to get creative, it **is** attainable. So, essentially what that did for me was reprogram my foggy misbeliefs. Ones that I've acquired over the years and formed the fear in the first place. It was just the way I interpreted my own life experiences. I knew my mom worked hard, especially after my dad died. She worked three jobs to maintain her family's financial needs. In the eyes of the impressionable teenager I was, I translated this into "The harder you work, the less time you spend with your family."

10. **Fear of Pissing People Off** – Of course you wouldn't do this intentionally. But sometimes, the people around you won't always agree with you or what you're doing. You've got to be ok with rocking the boat every now and then.

11. **Fear of Not Meeting Your Own Expectations** - This is a vicious cycle and it's another sticky one because who's in charge of defining those expectations? Us? Well, we're in trouble then because we've already learned that we're too tough on ourselves. Rarely do we ever feel we've met our own personal standards. This often comes from a need to please others, forcing us to try to live according to everybody else's rules.

12. **Fear of Hurting Someone's Feelings** - If we know that we're responsible for our own feelings then nobody can make us feel a certain way. Holding back the way we feel for the sake of someone else's feelings squashes our own inner truths and diminishes who we really are. How often do you push down your feelings and avoid speaking up? While we would never want to maliciously or deliberately hurt another, we can communicate effectively, lovingly, and honestly. If along the way we hurt someone's feeling through that process, that's not on our shoulders. They can choose to take it how they want to take it. It sounds harsh, but it's the truth. At least we give them the opportunity to choose, rather than holding back in fear of hurting their feelings.

13. **Fear of Being Rejected** - This is another painful one. If we've been rejected enough by our peers, our partners, or even our family members it can hurt. We can take it personally and may end up carrying with the belief that it's our fault; we're "defective" and "we're broken". There is something "wrong" with us. But, in fact, when we're rejected, it often has nothing to do with us. It has to do with the other person and where they are on their path. It's just a matter of shifting our perception of how we look at the "rejection".

Obviously there are plenty of other fears, but these are the most common.

So, what if we continued to peel back the layers of this whole fear thing? What do you think would be behind each and every one of them?

"A lack of self-love is behind your every fear."

You've got to come back to your original state, the person you were before life happened; before life gave you the challenges.

Who you truly are underneath all that "stuff", is who you really are!

You are enough. Just being yourself is the most authentic way to live.

So, the next time those fears try to get in the way of love and success just be willing to challenge them.

Stand up to them rather than believing everything they tell you.

Like forgiveness, this is a process and it takes practice. Courage is a muscle and like any muscle you have to be willing to flex that muscle every now and then.

Be willing to kick your fears out of the driver's seat.

Like I stated earlier, the most successful people in the world *have* experienced fear.

But, they've also learned to manage their fears.

The next time fears get a hold you, let them be an indicator that you're standing on the edge of the life you've known. It doesn't mean you can't do something. It just means you haven't done it yet.

"YET" is the keyword here.

Achieving our dreams and goals is going to require us to step outside our comfort zone and negative thinking patterns. It's going to require us to try new things, be uncomfortable, and be *okay* with being uncomfortable. That's why it's so important to have some type of roadmap, vision or goal sheet; so when we're scared we can put our attention on all the things we want, not on all the things we fear.

We've got to be willing to take the necessary steps regardless of having fear and we must learn how to do things even when we're afraid.

When I first began speaking in front of a group, I was scared to death.

But now that I've flexed that muscle enough times, it's not so scary anymore.

Although to some degree, fear is still present when I walk out onto that stage or in front of a group, I do it anyway.

Why? Because I want to share my message and help others more than I want to allow my fears to hold me back.

But, the beauty of it all is that the life we want, the life we are yearning for and the life we would **love** is just outside that comfort zone.

You've got to remember and believe that.

Rather than asking *"Am I good enough?"* Ask, *"How bad do I want it?"*

CHAPTER 10
Acceptance

"God, grant me the serenity to accept the things I cannot change, the courage to change the things I can and the wisdom to know the difference."

This is one of my most favorite prayers.

I recently reminded myself of this prayer when I noticed that little thing called "guilt" starting to creep in. I was on the road, making my two and half-hour drive back home. I had been out of town for two days taking care of some business matters and spending time with my mom.

As I drove home, the voice first started as just a whisper. *"I have so many things to do. How am I going to get them all done by the end of the week....?"*

Blah blah blah.

The farther I drove and the closer I got to home, the louder they became.

It wasn't long before I noticed I was becoming exceptionally anxious and annoyed. My tolerance for the traffic was decreasing by the second. I can't stand feeling negative emotions or being in a bad mood.

I try to do whatever I can to catch myself before I spiral downwards.

There's no room for bad moods in my life, they're life-suckers.

Fortunately, I've been doing this long enough that I immediately (well most times), do something about them and do what I can to move into a better feeling mood.

So, in this case, I challenged my soon- to-be bad mood.

As I reflected back on my recent thought patterns, I could clearly see why I felt the negative emotions. In that moment of awareness, I interrupted the voice and recited my prayer because it would do me no good to stress about something I couldn't change.

I couldn't change the fact that I had to be in the car for another two and a half hours. Nor could I change the fact that I had some business matters to take care of.

Plus, why would I ever want to look down upon the opportunity to spend quality time I got to spend with my mom?

Remember how I told you earlier there's a blessing in every perceivable challenge? Well, in this particular example, my so-called "challenge", was time; or lack thereof.

After I became aware of my thoughts, what was I to do next?

Control my thoughts, not my circumstances.

I had to flip the script.

The goal for me was to look for the hidden blessings within the challenge at hand.

Sometimes this is easy to do, other times it's a bit more challenging.

Although, the more you practice, the easier it gets.

In this particular example, my hidden blessing was the drive. Those miles in the car gave me five full hours of laser-focused, uninterrupted business education. I listened to podcasts and YouTube training videos the entire time. Something I had been putting off for quite some time.

I never would have listened to all of that if it wasn't for my trip. I educated myself and I made good use of my time so it wasn't "wasted".

Acceptance, like forgiveness, is an ongoing process. Acceptance was something I knew nothing about until my dad died. I was forced to practice it, and as I got older, I learned to accept the things I could not change.

Well, for the most part anyway.

It took me many years to accept my dad's choice. But I only could accept it as best as I could at the time.

It helped to rely heavily on the fact that everything happened for a reason too.

I know I've said this throughout the book, but I'll say it again; inner peace is a way of being, not a change of circumstances.

If we *wait* to be peaceful until everything is in "perfect" order, we could be waiting for a very, very long time. We could also be miserable in the meantime too.

Inner peace really boils down to accepting where you are, in this present moment.

I think we would agree the circumstances of our lives mainly consist of people and things.

Much of the time, we can't control either of those things either. But, then there are those times we can.

When you throw your hands up in the air just accept the way things are right now, you're not ignoring, excusing, or explaining it.

You are simply accepting the way things are in this one particular moment in time.

It could also be said that you are accepting the will of your Higher Power i.e. God, Jesus, Buddha, Universe. What or who is behind it is not of importance. What is important is that you trust and know in your heart there is a reason for going through what you're going through right now.

If you look back at your life, specifically the tough and tragic times, you will probably see how somehow, someway, there was a happy ending to many of the events you deemed as tragic or tough.

Being "happy" means that you can't always have things your way because there's a bigger picture. A divine picture, a plan that is so much greater than yours.

Much of our suffering comes from trying to rebel against that plan and refusing to look ahead.

Years ago, my car was broken down and we knew we weren't going to have the money to fix it for another month because it was a few thousand dollars.

I had two choices:

1. I could choose to throw a hissy fit and start barking about the inconvenience. I could carry on and on about how tragic it was to not have two cars and focus on our lack of money.

<u>OR</u>

2. I could feel blessed for the fact that we at least had one good car. I could focus on the fact that the kids schools were right around the corner, allowing us the opportunity to walk or ride our bikes to school. I could turn my eyes to the blessing of *not* having a car – and the chance it gave me to do a lot of writing because I was essentially confined to the house most of the day.

To ease our suffering, we must remind ourselves that there's a reason to everything.

I have a mantra I've been using for a while now, surely you've heard it: *"It is what it is"*.

I say it all the time, especially when things don't go my way and I'm on the verge of being a brat about it. Once I say it, I'm reassured that all will be well. It's as if the load drops from my shoulders and a sense of peace washes over me.

Another great mantra to adopt in difficult times is *"All is well."*

Write it on an index card or tape it to your bathroom mirror to serve as a constant reminder that all really is well.

There are many people who view suffering as a form of some punishment from God.

I think our "suffering" and the challenges we face often helps to keep us grounded. They humble us. They bring us reverence for life, for ourselves, and for others.

Contentment:

Here's a scenario: Baby grabs sparkling scissors. Mommy takes sparkling scissors away from baby. Baby screams because mommy won't let him play with the sparkling scissors. Baby is pissed because he can't have what he wants. Baby is learning that life isn't about getting what he wants; it's about being content and enjoying the things he does have.

As grown-ups, we are guilty of the same thing, only we want bigger toys. If we're only happy when we get what we want, then the majority of our lives will be filled with disappointments and we'll be discontent most of the time.

Essentially if we continue to live this way, our happiness will be dependent upon outside circumstances that most of the time, we don't even have control over.

So, the key to happiness and peace isn't ultimately about getting what we want, but learning to enjoy where we are and what we currently have.

We have to practice finding something enjoyable in any situation.

If we simply can't find anything at all, then we must rely on acceptance.

It's all about that "big picture". There are many things off our radar that we are not yet privy to. It's supposed to be that way. Only our highest self knows what is best for us in any given moment.

If we could just relax and trust that things will work out. While at the same time, understanding things may not work out the way *we* had in mind, but rather, in the bigger picture.

Instead of insisting you "drive the car", get your butt out of the driver's seat and into the passenger seat and enjoy the scenery as you let your highest self/God drive.

Rather than praying for the things you want, hand the power over to your highest self.

Example: If you're working at a company that is going through several layoffs, and you're petrified of losing your job and as a result, you're praying your little heart out not to lose your job…

Instead of praying not to lose your job, you could say something along the lines of *"Dear God, do what is best for all concerned."*

This allows you to accept where you are and allows the work of the highest self/God to be done. Which, it may turn out that you lose your job, but only to get an even better one.

You've got nothing to lose when you give up the control; your higher-self won't do a worse job of running your life than you will.

When you wake up each morning, step aside and allow your higher-self to drive for the day. Ask God to guide you.

Practice accepting everything that comes your way today. Just for one day, try not rebel against anything at all.

Going back to the example of my long drive home, momentarily I thought *I* knew what was best. I felt I "should be" working, and writing and doing all the busyness of my business. But, let's be real, do I *really* know what's best. There was a reason I heard the content I heard on the podcast I was listening to. I needed to hear those things so I could implement them into my business.

It was all part of the bigger picture.

Sometimes I get caught up and wish I was farther ahead than where I am today.

I'm the type of person that once my mind is made up and I decide to go after what I want, I want it right *now*.

Actually, if I'm being totally honest, I want it *yesterday*!

This personality trait is a blessing in the sense that once I decide to go for something, I'm unstoppable. When there's a long process or a learning curve involved though, patience becomes a curse. I've been known to say *"I just want to hit the fast forward button!"*

When it came to my business journey, I've had to learn some fundamental lessons along the way. Although frustrating at times, my only choice was and will always be to accept where I am in this very moment and continue to move forward.

Now, contentment and acceptance is not to be confused with "laziness". Acceptance doesn't give us a ticket to sit on our butts and cry "Woe is me" from the hilltops.

We must continue to take action.

The serenity prayer doesn't say "Accept the things you can change." *Rather*, it says *"give me the courage to change the things I can."* Acceptance means you continue to move forward as much as you possibly can.

Final Words of Wisdom

I believe in you. You are Divine.

You were built to love and be loved. You were built for greatness.

You are way more courageous and resilient than you think.

Stepping into your greatness doesn't mean achieving some unachievable standard. It just means you strive to be the best you can be. You no longer allow yourself to play small in any area of your life.

It will require you to not only be determined, but persistent and kind to yourself throughout your journey.

You will have your fair share of "off-days" where you don't feel like putting your best-self forward.

Don't let those days to stand in your way. A brighter day awaits you tomorrow. Be willing to move forward despite of where you were yesterday.

Achieving greatness will require you to wake up each day and face your fears and do what is hard, but vitally necessary.

You have so many untapped gifts, talents and love to share. Believe you're worth every single one of them as they are revealed to you.

Recap

Let's finish up by going over the new techniques and practices to keep in your back pocket. They are:

1. Learn to love yourself.
2. Become self-aware.
3. Take charge of your own well-being.
4. Let go of your guilt.
5. Learn from others.
6. Be in the moment.
7. See yourself through the eyes of others.
8. Forgive yourself and others.
9. Overcome your fears.
10. Acceptance

I hope these tools will light your path to the same contentment and happiness I've found. Although our journeys will never end, it will always be so much more fulfilling and joyous than before.

Be well, be easy on yourself and always, always, love yourself.

With love and appreciation,

~Jody

Works Cited

Kam, K. (2014). *Web Md*. Retrieved November 16, 2014, from Web Md: http://www.webmd.com/balance/stress-management/features/how-anger-hurts-your-heart

Disclaimer

Although the author has made every effort to ensure that the information in this book was correct at press time, the author does not assume and hereby disclaim any liability to any party for any loss, damage, or disruption caused by errors or omissions, whether such errors or omissions result from negligence, accident, or any other cause. The reader should regularly consult a physician in matters relating to his/her health and particularly with respect to any symptoms that may require diagnosis or medical attention.